AF684238

LAWS

OF

THE CHOCTAW NATION

PASSED AT THE

REGULAR SESSION OF THE GENERAL COUNCIL

CONVENED AT

TUSHKA HUMMA

OCTOBER 6, 1890, ADJOURNED NOVEMBER 14, 1890.

LAWS

OF THE

CHOCTAW NATION

MADE AND ENACTED BY THE.

GENERAL COUNCIL,

FROM

1886 TO 1890 INCLUSIVE.

LAWS

OF

THE CHOCTAW NATION

PASSED AT THE

SPECIAL SESSION OF THE GENERAL COUNCIL

CONVENED AT

TUSHKA HUMMA

APRIL 6, 1891, ADJOURNED APRIL 11, 1891

SR Scholarly Resources Inc.
1508 Pennsylvania Avenue · Wilmington, Delaware 19806

E
99
C8
C577
1975

SCHOLARLY RESOURCES, INC.
Wilmington, Delaware • London

Reprint edition published in 1975

Library of Congress Catalog Card Number: 75-3688
ISBN: 0-8420-1879-4

Manufactured in the United States of America

LAWS

OF

THE CHOCTAW NATION

PASSED AT THE

REGULAR SESSION OF THE GENERAL COUNCIL

CONVENED AT

TUSHKA HUMMA

OCTOBER 6, 1890, ADJOURNED NOVEMBER 14, 1890.

LAWS

OF

THE CHOCTAW NATION

REGULAR SESSION, 1890.

NO. 1.

A resolution accepting the reports of Turner B. Turnbull. District Trustee of 3rd District. C. N.

To the General Council:

We, your committee to whom was referred the report of Turner B. Turnbull, have carefully examined the same and find it to be true and correct, with the balance on hand amounting to $2,119.70, and ask the adoption of the following bill, to-wit:

Be it resolved by the General Council of the Choctaw Nation assembled; That the report of Turner B. Turnbull, District Trustee, 3rd District, C. N., be and is hereby accepted as being true and correct, and that this resolution shall take effect and be in force from and after its passage.

Approved Oct. 11, 1890.

W. N. JONES, P. C. C. N.

NO. 2.

TUSHKA HUMMA, I. T.

Whereas, it has pleased the Almighty to remove from our midst our esteemed friends and staunch adherents and supporters of the Choctaw and Chickasaw Government, the Hon. Jos. P. Folsom and Hon. Peter E. Noel and Hon. G. W. Harkins and Hon. John Williams and Hon Ibayonubbee. And while we bow in humble submission to the wise dispensation of Him who controls the Universe, yet we mourn the loss of five who so long served their people faithfully and always had the interest of their people at heart; therefore,

Be it resolved by the General Council of the Choctaw Nation assembled, that both houses of the General Council adjourn for four days, from Thursday, Oct. 16th, 1890, at 3 o'clock p. m., until Monday, Oct. 20th, 1890, at 9 a. m., out of respect to the deceased above named; and that each member and all officers of the Council wear the usual badge of mourning for thirty days and that the National Secretary is hereby authorized to send a copy of this resolution to the bereaved families of the above named deceased.

And be it futher resolved that members of the General Council and all friends of the deceased meet in the Representative Hall at 3:30 o'clock p. m., Oct. 16th, 1890, for memorial services.

And that this resolution shall take effect and be in force from and after its passage.

Approved Oct. 15th, 1890.

W. N. JONES, P. C. C. N.

NO. 3.

Be it resolved by the Council of the Choctaw Nation assembled; That the sum of fifty dollars be and is hereby appropriated out of any money in the treasury not otherwise appropriated, to pay Judge C. S. Vinson for services in superintending the building of jail in the third District of the Choctaw Nation, at the Circuit Court ground, as provided for in the act of 1886, providing for jails in that district of the Choctaw Nation, and the National Auditor is hereby authorized to issue his warrant on the National Treasurer for the same, and this resolution shall take effect and be in force from and after its passage.

Approved Oct. 21, 1890.

W. N. JONES, P. C. C. N.

NO. 4.

A resolution accepting the report of Charles Winston, District Trustee, 2d District.

Your committee to whom was referred the report of Charles Winston, has carefully examined the same and find it to be true and correct, with the balance on hand amounting to $587.29; also find that outstanding certificates of $175.70, and respectfully ask the adoption of following resolution, to-wit:

Be it resolved by the General Council of the Choctaw Nation assembled, that the report of Charles Winston, District Trustee 2d District, be and the same is hereby accepted as being true and correct.

Be it further resolved, that the District Trustee of the 2d District is hereby authorized to pay the outstanding certificate of $175.70 out of the balance on hand, and that this resolution shall take effect and be in force from and after its passage.

Approved Oct. 22, 1896.

W. N. JONES, P. C. C. N.

NO. 5.

A resolution accepting the report of John P. Turnbull, Superintendent of Public Instruction, C. N.

To the General Council:

Your committee on schools, to whom was referred the report of J. P. Turnbull, Superintendent of Public Instruction, C. N., find the same to be true and correct, with the balance on hand amounting to $1,350.78, contigent fund on hand 16 cents, and ask the passage of the following resolution, to-wit:

SECTION 1. Be it resolved by the General Council of the Choctaw Nation assembled, that the report of John P. Turnbull, Superintendent of Public Instruction, be and the same is hereby accepted as being true and correct, and that this resolution shall take effect and be in force from and after its adoption.

Approved Oct. 22, 1890.

W. N. JONES, P. C. C. N.

NO. 6.

TUSHKA HUMMA, C. N., Oct. 15, 1890.

The Senate and House of Representatives, Choctaw Nation, in General Council assembled.

Your committee, to whom was referred the report of S. E. Lewis, District Collector, C. N., finds that he collected for the fiscal year, ending July 31, 1890, ($6,554.31) six thousand five hundred and fifty-four and 31-100 dollars, and that he has satisfactorily reported and accounted for the same; therefore

Be it resolved by the General Council of the Choctaw Nation assembled, that the report of S. E. Lewis, District Collector, 1st District, C. N., be accepted as correct, and this resolution be in force from and after its passage.

Approved Oct. 23, 1890.

W. N. JONES, P. C. C. N.

NO. 7.

To the General Council:

We, your committee to whom was referred the report of Ben Hampton, National Inspector on the Missouri, Kansas & Texas line of railroad, have thoroughly examined same and beg leave to submit the following resolution and ask its adoption:

Be it resolved by the General Council of the Choctaw Nation assembled, that the report of Ben Hampton, National Inspector on the M. K. & T. line of railroad, be accepted as true and correct, and this resolution shall take effect and be in force from and after its passage.

Approved Oct 23, 1890.

W. N. JONES, P. C. C. N.

NO. 8.

To the General Council:

Your committee, to whom was referred the report of B. F. Smallwood, Principal Chief, C. N., in regard to the disbursement of contingent fund, after having examined the same would beg leave to submit the following resolution, to-wit:

SECTION 1. Be it resolved by the General Council of the Choctaw Nation assembled, that the report of B. F. Smallwood for contingent fund be and the same is hereby accepted as being true and correct, and this resolution shall take effect and be in force from and after its passage.

Approved Oct. 24, 1890.

W. N. JONES, P. C. C. N.

NO. 9.

An act relating to the accounts of Peter Garland, District Trustee for First District, C. N.

Whereas, the accounts of Peter Garland, District Trustee, First District, C. N., are in such confusion as to make it impossible properly to balance the same, and

Whereas, there appears to be outstanding unsatisfied certificates of said Peter Garland amounting to the sum of $1,281.25.

Now, therefore, be it enacted by the General Council of the Choctaw Nation assembled:

1. That the District Attorney for said First District is hereby instructed to proceed at once by law against said Peter Garland and his sureties on his bond for the collection of said sum and all proper costs, and that the money so collected be turned into the National Treasury for National purposes.

2. In order to make good the deficiency caused by said outstanding certificates and to pay the same, there is hereby appropriated out of any funds in the Treasury not otherwise appropriated, the sum of $1,281.25, and that the National Treasurer of the Choctaw Nation is hereby authorized to pay the same on presenting the certificates, and that this act shall take effect and be in force from and after its passage.

Approved Oct. 25, 1890.

W. N. JONES, P. C. C. N.

NO. 10.

An act granting Lewis Lucas the right to establish a toll gate at the old iron bridge ford on the road leading from Fort Smith to Eufaula.

Be it enacted by the General Council of the Choctaw Nation assembled, that Lewis Lucas is hereby granted the privilege of establishing a toll gate at or near the old iron bridge ford on San Bois on the road leading from Fort Smith, Ark., to Eufaula; Creek Nation, I. T., upon the following terms and conditions to-wit: Said Lucas shall put and keep in good repair and fit for (vehicle) travel said road for a distance of five miles on each side of said ford, for which services he shall be allowed to charge all persons passing on the same, except citizens of this Nation, the following rates of toll:

For each four (4) wheeled vehicle, drawn by four (4) or more horses, mules or cattle with driver, 50 cents; for each four (4) wheeled vehicle, drawn by one or two horses, mules or cattle with driver, 25 cents; for man and horse, 10 cents; each person, foot, 5 cents; for each animal in any drove of horses, cattle, hogs, sheep or mules per head, 1 cent.

SEC. 2. The privilege to receive toll as above shall not take effect until said road is put in repair, and shall continue for ten (10) years from said time, provided said road is kept in good repair.

SEC. 3. That if any non-citizen refuse to pay the tolls above provided for, upon application, with proper proof, being made to the United States Indian Agent for the Choctaws, he shall take such steps as may be necessary to collect the same.

SEC. 4. This act shall take effect from and after its passage and approval.

Approved Oct. 25, 1890.

W. N. JONES, P. C. C. N.

NO. 11.

An act relating to citizens of the Choctaw Nation taking the oath of allegiance to the Uniten States,

Be it enacted by the General Council of the Choctaw Nation assembled, that any member of the Choctaw tribes of Indians, either by blood, adoption or marriage into said tribe, and subject to the government of the Choctaw Nation, who has taken or may hereafter take the oath of allegiance to the government of the United States, shall be disqualified to hold any office of trust or profit in the Choctaw Nation, and to vote at any election in said Nation, and to be impaneled as a juror in any court under the government of said Choctaw Nation.

This act shall take effect from and after its passage.

Approved Oct. 25, 1890.

W. N. JONES, P. C. C. N.

NO. 12.

An act establishing the citizenship of Martha Beals and others.

Be it enacted by the General Council of the Choctaw Nation assembled, that the citizenship of the following named persons is hereby established, to-wit: Martha Beals and her husband, Andrew Beals, and their children, Reuben, Missouri, Pinksey, Margaret, Andy, Becky, Thomas, Beel and Bill Beals, and they are hereby declared citizens of the Choctaw Nation and entitled to all the rights and privileges and immunities of such.

This act shall take effect upon its passage and approval.

Approved Oct. 25, 1890.

W. N. JONES, P. C. C. N.

NO. 13.

An act making appropriation for taking care of and furnishing repairs for Capitol building.

Be it enacted by the General Council of the Choctaw Nation assembled, that the sum of eighty-nine and 65-100 dollars is hereby appropriated to pay Edward Spring for taking care of the Capitol and furnishing locks, etc., for building.

That the National Auditor issue his warrant on the National Treasurer for the above amount, and that the Treasurer pay the same, and that this act take effect and be in force from and after its passage.

Approved Oct. 25, 1890.

W. N. JONES, P. C. C. N.

NO. 14.

A resolution accepting the report of C. J. Ralston, Superintendent of Armstrong Orphan School, C. N.

To the General Council:

Your committee, to whom was referred the report of C. J. Ralston, Superintendent of Armstrong Orphan School, find the same to be true and correct, and ask the passage of the following resolution, to-wit:

SEC. 1. Be it resolved by the General Council of the Choctaw Nation assembled, that the report of C. J. Ralston, Superintendent of Armstrong Orphan School, be and the same is hereby accepted as being true and correct, with the balance on hand amounting to $941.89; and that this resolution shall take effect and be in force from and after its passage.

Approved Oct. 27, 1890.

W. N. JONES, P. C. C. N.

NO. 15.

A resolution stating the time for electing Superintendent of Public Schools and District Trustees.

Be it resolved by the General Council of the Choctaw Nation assembled, that the Senate and House of Representatives shall meet in joint session on Wednesday, the 29th of October, 1890, at 10 o'clock a. m., in the Representative Hall for the purpose of electing the superintendent of Public Schools and District Trustees, and this resolution take effect and be in force from and after its passage.

Approved Oct. 28, 1890.

W. N. JONES, P. C. C. N.

NO. 16.

An act recognizing certain persons as citizens of this Nation.

Be it enacted be the General Council of the Choctaw Nation assembled, that Sandos Amos, his wife Ann, and William Amos, and Solomon Wilson and wife and their four children, all full blood Choctaws and lately come to this Nation from Mississippi, be and they are hereby recognized as citizens of the Choctaw Nation, and entitled to all the rights, privileges and immunities of citizens, and this act shall take effect and be in force from and after its passage.

Approved Oct, 29, 1890.

W. N. JONES, P. C. C. N.

NO. 17.

An act conferring citizenship on certain persons named.

Be it enacted by the General Council of the Choctaw Nation assembled, that Sexton Amos, Mat Sukke, Amos Bell, Jimson Bell, John Alusion, Sarah Wilson, Isaac Wilson, Mary Wilson, Eve Wilson, Horace Wilson, Thompson Barney, Isaac Simpson, and Tom Yark, all late of the State of Mississippi, are hereby recognized as citizens of this Nation, and entitled to all the rights, privileges and immunities of citizens of this Nation, and this act shall take effect and be in force from and after its passage.

Approved Oct. 30, 1890.

W. N. JONES, P. C. C. N.

NO. 18.

Amendment to Section 2 of the act of Nov. 1, 1882, in regard to shipping hay.

Be it enacted by the General Council of the Choctaw Nation assembled, that from and after the passage of this act a royalty is hereby levied on all prairie or wild grass of one dollar ($1.00) per ton for each ton of such grass cut for sale or barter, whether upon the public domain or within citizens' enclosures.

The sheriff of each county shall collect said royalty and pay the same, less 10 per cent. for his services, to the County Treasurer for county purposes of the county in which such grass shall have been cut.

Nothing herein contained as to impose a royalty on grass cut by any citizen for his own use, and this act take effect from and after its passage.

Approved Oct. 30, 1890.

W. N. JONES, P. C. C. N.

NO. 19.

An act to abolish Good Spring and Cole Spring precincts in Blue County, and to establish Jones precinct instead.

Be it enacted by the Gnneral Council of the Choctaw Nation assembled, that Good Spring precinct and Cole Spring precinct, located in Blue county, be and the same are hereby abolished. Be it further enacted, that an election precinct is hereby established at Cornelius Jones' house, in Blue county, and shall be called and known as Jones precinct; and voters may vote at said precinct, and this act shall take effect and be in force from and after its passage.

Approved Oct. 30, 1890.

W. N. JONES, P. C. C. N.

NO. 20.

An act changing boundary lines of certain counties.

Be it enacted by the General Council of the Choctaw Nation assembled, that boundary line of Wade county shall be as follows, to-wit: Beginning on the top of the dividing ridge where boundary line of Mosholetubbe district strikes the boundary line of the state of Arkansas, running thence along the top of the dividing ridge westward to where the road leading from Horse Prairie to Fort Smith crosses the same; thence along said road to Jack's Fork; thence down Jack's Fork to its junction with Kiamitia; thence down Kiamitia to the narrows, one mile above Hotoka's place; thence on a straight line to a spring on the Kiamitia Mountain, known as Okchaga's place; thence following a line on the top of the main Kiamitia Mountain eastwardly to the Arkansas line; thence along said line northwardly to the beginning.

SEC. 2. Be it further enacted that the boundary lines of Cedar county are hereby changed so that it will follow up Ward's Creek to its junction with Little River to the source of said Ward's Creek; thence in a northwardly direction on a straight line to the top of the main Kiamitia Mountain to a junction with Wade county lines, and all that portion of Wade county under the old boundaries east of Ward's Creek and the line from its source to the top of Kiamitia Mountain is hereby declared a part of Washoba county, and all that portion on the west of said Ward's Creek and line is hereby declared a part of Cedar county.

SEC. 3. Be it enacted that all former laws are hereby repealed, and this act take effect and be in force from and after its passage.

Approved Oct. 31, 1890.

W. N. JONES, P. C. C. N.

NO. 21.

An act relating to the school system of the Choctaw Nation.

Be it enacted by the General Council of the Choctaw Nation assembled.

BOARD OF EDUCATION.

CHAP. I. SEC. 1. There is hereby created a Board of Education of the Choctaw Nation, to be composed of the Principal Chief, who shall be ex-officio President of said Board, one Superintendent of Schools and three (3) District Trustees, one from each District. The Superintendent of schools, and the District Trustees shall be elected by both houses of the General Council in joint session; shall hold office for the term of two years, and until their successors are qualified, and shall receive for compensation an annual salary as follows: The Superintendent, six hundred dollars ($600); each District Trustee, four hundred dollars ($400); to be paid quarterly out of the general funds of the Nation.

SEC. 2. Said Superintendent and District Trustees shall each, before entering upon the duties of their respective offices, give bond to the Choctaw Nation with at least two good sureties, in the sum of five thousand dollars ($5000), to be approved by the Principal Chief, conditioned upon the faithful performance of all duties imposed on them by law. They shall each take the usual oath of officers of the Choctaw Nation.

SEC. 3. The powers and duties of the Board of Education shall be as follows, to-wit:

1. To exercise a general supervisory control over the school system of the Choctaw Nation.

2. To make all necessary rules and regulations, not inconsistent with this act, for its own government and the govern-

ment of the various Academies, Seminaries and neighborhood schools.

3. To examine and appoint all teachers as hereinafter provided.

4. To contract with Superintendents of public schools; but no such contract shall be valid unless approved by the Principal Chief, and signed by at least three other members of the Board.

5. To revoke the certificate of any teacher for immoral, intemperate or improper conduct,

6. To prescribe the text books to be used in all schools.

7. To suspend any Academy or Seminary in case of general sickness or epidemic.

8. To discontinue any neighborhood school, should the same in their judgment be expedient.

9. To designate permanent locations for any or all the neighborhood schools, if in their judgment such action would promote the cause of education. Powers in paragraphs 8 and 9 may be delegated to respective District Trustees.

10. To prescribe the course of study in the various public schools, and it is made the duty of the Board to foster as far as possible, in the Academies, manual training in the mechanical arts and theoretical and practical agriculture.

11. To select scholars to be sent to the states to school at public expense; such scholars must be selected from those in attendance upon public schools; they shall be selected from the various districts as nearly as may be in proportion to the school population of each, and the number of each sex shall be kept equal. They shall be examined by some competent physician, selected by the Superintendent of schools, and if physically disqualified, shall be rejected and others sent in the stead of such as may be rejected.

The Board of Education shall have a seal with the inscription, "Board of Education, Choctaw Nation." It shall keep a record of its proceedings, and its official acts shall be authenticated by its seal.

SEC. 4. It shall be the duty of the Board of Education to select one Superintendent and at least two teachers for each public school now, or hereafter to be erected in the Choctaw Nation. Advertisements shall be inserted in papers in at least three different states and in one paper in the Choctaw Nation, setting forth the duties, qualifications and emoluments of such

Superintendents and teachers, other things being equal, preference shall be given to applicants professing Christianity. The teachers shall have had at least 10 years experience in their profession, and must bring ample testmonials as to competency and morality. The male teachers must be graduates of some college of established reputation and capable of giving instruction in Greek, Latin, German and French. The female must be graduates of some higher institution of learning or some reputable normal school, and capable of instructing in two modern languages other than English. Upon the approval of this act, it shall be the duty of the Superintendent of schools at once to notify the Superintendent of public schools in writing, that the Choctaw Nation elect to cancel all existing contracts at the expiration of the current scholastic year. He shall then begin to negotiate for new contracts. As to Academies, Seminaries or High Schools hereafter to be established, contracts will be made in accordance with the first paragraph of this Section and Section 5 of this chapter.

2. As to public schools now in existence: The Board of Education may in its discretion, make contracts as heretofore subject to the general provisions of this act, with Boards of Home Missions, in which latter event, however, paragraph one of this Section and Section 5 of this Chapter shall not apply, nor will the Nation engage to pay the salaries of Superintendents or teacher in such schools. Such contracts shall also contain a clause authorizing either party to rescind the same upon six months' notice in writing to the other, and the absence of such stipulations shall render such contract void *ab initio.*

SEC. 5. The Superintendent of each of the public schools shall receive an annual salary of $1,200, to be paid in equal quarterly installments out of the general funds of the Choctaw Nation. The teachers in said public schools shall receive each an annual salary of not less than $750 and not more than $1,200, to be paid in like manner out of said general funds. The Superintendents shall hold their positions for six years, and the Board is authorized to make written contracts to that effect. Any Superintendent or teacher, may, however be discharged upon charges sustained by the Board; but such charges must be in writing; must be heard by the full Board. The party charged must have written notice of the time and place of investigation and given full opportunity to be heard in his or her own defense, and at least four members of the Board must concur in sustaining the charge and charges.

SEC. 6. All sums appropriated for the support and maintenance of the public schools shall be paid out to the respective Superintendents in equal installments on the first Mondays in September, November, February and May of each year. The Superintendent of schools shall make his requisition for such sums, under direction of the Board, upon the National Auditor, who shall thereupon issue his warrant for the same, said warrants shall be paid out of the respective appropriations by National Treasurer, any surplus remaining over at the expiration of the scholastic year, shall be returned by the the Superintendent in whose schools such surplus shall exist, to the National Treasurer, and by him converted into the treasury. This section shall apply to all new contracts whatever with Superintendents of Public Schools.

SEC. 7. The Board of Education shall examine all applicants for the position of teacher in the neighborhood schools, but for this purpose the Principal Chief and each District Trustee may each select a proxy to represent him at such examination. Such proxies need not be citizens of the Choctaw Nation, but must be competent to conduct such examination. The applicants shall be examined in Reading, Writing, Spelling and Grammar of the English language, in Geography and History, particularly of the United States; a fair knowledge of the Constitution of the United States and of the Choctaw Nation shall also be required. It is particularly enjoined upon the Board, in selecting teachers, that regard be had to the disposition of applicants as far as the same can be determined by personal observation at the time of such examination. Upon the conclusion of the examination in each district, each successful candidate shall be required, according to merit into one of the three grades to be known as "First," "Second" and "Third" Grades, the first being the highest. Each successful candidate shall receive a certificate from the Board, specifying his or her grade. Teachers shall be assigned by the Board, as near as may be, to the neighborhood school whence they are sent by the respective local trustees; but if any local trustee fails to send a candidate, or having sent one, such candidate fails to secure a certificate, then the Board shall send some other competent person to such neighborhood. The foregoing examination shall be conducted at least once in each district annually, and for their services in this behalf the members of the Board doing the actual labor, shall receive each the sum of $5.00 per day and mileage at the rate of five (5) cents per mile for each mile actually traveled. Such examinations shall not be held more than five (5) days each year in each district. The times and places of such examinations shall be fixed previously by the Board, and at least three months notice given thereof by advertisement in one newspaper published in the Nation, the contingent fund of the Superintendent of Schools.

SEC. 8. The scholastic year of the public schools shall begin on the first Monday in September of each year and shall close between the 10th and 30th of June. The Superintendent of schools and three District Trustees shall attend the annual examination of each of said schools; and to this end the Board of Education shall, by regulation, fix the dates of the closing thereof in such wise as to enable said Superintendent and District Trustees to be personally present at all of said examinations.

SEC. 9. The Superintendent of schools shall have an annual contingent fund $450 and each District Trustee of $750, for the expenditure of which they must account to the full Board of Education at its annual meeting. All minor expenses not herein specifically provided for shall be paid out of the respective contingent funds.

SEC. 10. The full Board of Education shall meet at least once in every year in regular annual session. This meeting shall be at Tushka Humma and shall begin during the first week of the regular annual session of the General Council; at such meeting the Board shall make up its annual report to said Council. Such report shall contain an itemized account of all expenditures on account of schools by said Board or any of its members. It shall also contain a general review of the last scholastic year, the condition, progress and attendance at all schools and such recommendations as to legislation as the Board may deem expedient or necessary. The Board shall transmit with its own report, the reports of the various Superintendents of public schools.

SEC. 11. The President may call special sessions of the Board whenever he shall deem it necessary, to be held at such place as he may designate.

SUPERINTENDENT OF SCHOOLS.

CHAP. II. SEC. 1. The Superintendent of schools shall be the executive officer of the Board of Education, and is charged with carrying into effect all orders, rules and regulations of said Board.

SEC. 2. He shall correspond with the principals of schools outside the Nation, at which Choctaw pupils are attending, at the public expense, and with the scholars themselves, in order to acquaint himself with the progress and needs of such scholars.

DISTRICT TRUSTEE.

CHAP. III. SEC. 1. Each District Trustee shall have a seal of office, which shall bear on the outer edge the words, "District Trustee, Choctaw Nation," and within the circle the Choctaw name of his district, followed by the word "District." As soon as qualified, each District Trustee shall write his signature in a book to be kept by National Treasurer for that purpose. All certificates required by law to be made by a District Trustee shall be signed in person and his seal of office affixed to the same.

SEC. 2. The teachers of neighborhood schools shall be paid by the National Treasurer, upon monthly certificates of the District Trustee of the district in which such shall be located. Such certificates shall be made out upon the monthly report of each teacher when certified to by the local Trustee. Each District Trustee shall file all certified teachers' reports and present the same to the Board at its annual meeting, with his district report.

SEC. 3. The District Trustees shall also report to the Board, at its regular annual meeting, the names of all the scholars as reported to them by the local Trustees.

SEC. 4. Each District Trustee shall have power to suspend any neighborhood school in his district in time of general sickness or epidemic in the neighborhood.

SEC. 5. The District Trustees shall, each in his own district, at once upon the receipt by him of any charges against any teacher in his district, to investigate the same, and if the charges are sustained to suspend the delinquent and appoint as a substitute any available person holding a certificate from the Board of Education.

LOCAL TRUSTEES.

CHAP. IV. Sec. 1. There shall be a Local Trustee in each neighborhood, who shall be the head of a family; shall be appointed by the District Trustee of his district; shall hold office for one scholastic year.

Sec. 2. It shall be the duty of the Local Trustee to select one competent person in his neighborhood who may be a non-citizen and send him or her to the annual teachers' examination in his district. He shall visit his school at least once a month, and at the end of each month he shall examine the teacher's report and account, and if the same be correct, he shall so certify. Such account and certificate shall be sent by the teacher to the District Trustee. He shall report to the District Trustee any improper conduct on the part of the teacher for investigation as provided in this act.

It shall be the duty of all Local Trustees to uphold teachers in enforcing proper discipline in the neighborhood school, and to enjoin upon pupils the necessity of showing due respect to the teacher.

Sec. 3. Local Trustees shall receive no compensation for their services.

Sec. 4. Local Trustees shall enroll all children in their respective neighborhoods between the ages of seven and eighteen, and report the same to the proper District Trustee at the end of each scholastic year.

NEIGHBORHOOD SCHOOLS.

CHAP. V. Sec. 1. Any neighborhood that can employ a teacher shall be entitled to a neighborhood school; provided, however, that such schools shall not be nearer to each other than three miles, measured along the most direct traveled wagon road; and provided further, that this limitation as to distance shall not apply to acknowledged towns. The provisions of this section are subject to the powers conferred upon the Board of Education by Sec. 3, par. 8 and 9, Chap. I., of this act.

Sec. 2. Neighborhood schools shall be taught at least six (6) hours daily, Saturdays and Sundays excepted, during the term, and shall have regular hours of opening and closing. They shall open for the term on the first Monday of September and close on the last day of May of each year; but the District Trustee shall have power to grant short vacations and holidays at stated times during the term.

SEC. 3. The benefits of a free neighborhood school shall extend only to such Choctaw children as attend the schools within the Choctaw Nation established; and it is hereby made the duty of all Choctaw parents or guardians to send their children to school.

SEC. 4. The parents or guardians of all enrolled children who fail to send them to school shall be fined ten cents per day for each child enrolled who shall fail in attendance (not, however to exceed $2.00 per child per month), except in cases of sickness, bad weather or other casualty. The money shall be collected as provided for in Sec. 5, Chap. VI, of this act, (but in no case shall any sum be paid out of the County Treasury on this account), shall be paid into the contingent fund of the District Trustee of that district. In case of necessity or other good cause shown to the District Trustee, he may excuse any child from attendance upon the neighborhood schools for reasonable periods of time.

SEC. 5. Teachers in neighborhood schools shall be entitled to two dollars ($2.00) per month for each scholar in attendance, when such scholar has attended more than twenty days in the month. But where the attendance has been less than twenty (20) days, then such teacher shall receive 10 cents for each day of attendance; *provided, however*, that the teachers of the First Grade shall not receive over forty-five dollars ($45) in any one month; those of the Second Grade not over thirty dollars ($30), and those of the Third Grade not over twenty dollars ($20).

SEC. 6. A scholastic month shall be taken and held to extend from a day of one calendar month to the corresponding day of the succeeding calendar month.

BOARDING SCHOOLS.

CHAP. VI. SEC. 1. The Superintendent of each boarding school in the Nation shall give a bond with at least two sureties, payable to the Principal Chief, and to be approved by him, in the sum of five thousand dollars ($5,000), conditioned upon the faithful performance of his duties as imposed by law, and observance of his contract with Board of Education.

SEC. 2. The Superintendents shall take charge of their respective schools and conduct the same under the supervision of the Board of Education. They shall make full reports to the Board at the end of each scholastic year, which reports shall embody the names and ages of all scholars, with their percentage in each study, the attendance and other matters connected with their progress and the internal discipline of the schools, together with an itemized statement of all moneys received and expended, accompanied with proper vouchers.

SEC. 3. The number of scholars at each of these schools shall be one hundred; at Spencer Academy they shall be boys, and at New Hope Seminary they shall be girls. One of each sex shall be chosen from the Choctaws residing in the Chickasaw country, ninety-nine of each sex shall be apportioned among the various counties of the Choctaw Nation by the Board of Education in proportion to the school population of said counties. The Board shall notify the County Judge of each County at least thirty days before the beginning of each scholastic year, how many pupils of each sex his county is entitled to; each County Judge shall then select his county's quota from the neighborhood schools, and give each person so selected, or to his or her parents or guardian, a certificate of such selection.

SEC. 4. Before admission each scholar shall be required to pass a creditable physical examination before some competent physician selected by the Superintendent of schools, and also a mental examination, the standard of which shall be fixed by the Board. There shall be no limit as to age, though a regular course shall be held to be five years, but any pupil may be retained longer or sooner discharged by the Board upon recommendation by the Superintendent of either school.

SEC. 5. Upon selecting the scholars from his county each Judge shall forthwith notify the proper Superintendent of public schools of names and postoffice address of such scholars, and also the name and address of the Sheriff of his county. If any pupil to whom a certificate has been issued shall fail for ten (10) days after the opening of school, or, when the certificate was issued after the opening of school, for ten days after the proper superintendent has been notified, to report to his or her school, it shall be the duty of the Superintendent of such school to notify the proper Sheriff of such failure. The sheriff shall at once investigate the case, and if the pupil was not detained by high water, or sickness of self or family, then he shall take such pupil within five days to the proper school at the expense of parent or guardian. For this duty he shall be allowed $2.00 per day and five cents per mile for each mile actually traveled by each student and by himself by the usual traveled route. The Sheriff's account must be verified under oath, and if on demand, the parent or guardian refuse to pay the same, the Sheriff may take summary judgement in the circuit court of his district, upon a satisfactory showing to the judge thereof, that the expenses were lawfully incurred, for the amount of his bill and costs, without further notice or demand against such parent or guardian. Upon such judgment execution shall issue forthwith. If such execution cannot be satisfied, then the Sheriff shall be paid out of the County Treasury where such execution debtor reside, upon the County Judge being satisfied of the correctness of the account. The county paying the account shall be subrogated to the Sheriff's rights under the execution. If there be more than one delinquent pupil in the same county, it shall be the duty of the Sheriff to take all such in one trip, and the circuit court shall not give judgment in any case where this provision appears not to have been complied with.

SEC. 6. No family shall have more than one scholar at any one time at the boarding schools of this Nation, nor in the States at the expense of the nation.

ORPHAN SCHOOLS.

CHAP. VII. SEC. 1. There shall be fifty (50) orphan boys at Armstrong Academy and fifty (50) girls at Wheelock Seminary. During vacation, such as have no relative or proper friends to visit, shall be cared for by respective Superintendents.

SEC. 2. There shall be no restriction as to age. The regular course shall be five years; but the Board in its direction may in particular cases order the retention or discharge of any pupil. No pupil shall be discharged except upon the order of the Board.

SEC. 3. The County Judges shall select the pupils, apportionment having been made by the Board of Education as provided for in the case of boarding schools. Regard shall be had in selections to the most needy, and more than one pupil may be sent from the same family.

SEC. 4. Each Sheriff shall collect all pupils and take them in one trip to the proper school. He shall be allowed $2.00 per day and actual necessary expenses, to be paid out of respective County Treasuries upon properly verified account.

SEC. 5. The Superintendents of orphan schools shall give a similar bond and shall report in like manner to the Board as prescribed in this act for Superintendents of boarding schools.

This act shall take effect from and after its passage and approval, and all other acts and parts of acts on the subject of schools are hereby repealed.

Approved Oct. 31, 1890.

W. N. JONES, P. C. C. N.

NO. 22.

A resolution accepting the report of Alfred Docking, Superintendent of Spencer Academy, C. N.

Your committee on schools, to whom was referred the report of Alfred Docking, Superintendent of Spencer Academy, have carefully examined the same and find it to be true and correct, "with no balance on hand," and ask the passage of the following resolution, to-wit:

Be it resolved by the General Council of the Choctaw Nation assembled, that the report of Alfred Docking, Superintendent of Spencer Academy, is hereby accepted as being true and correct, and that this resolution shall take effect and be in force from and after its passage.

Approved Oct. 31, 1890.

W. N. JONES, P. C. C. N.

NO. 23.

A resolution providing for the translating and binding in book form all the laws enacted by the several General Councils of the Choctaw Nation from 1886 to 1890.

Whereas, the laws of the Choctaw Nation enacted by the several Councils of 1886, 1887, 1888, 1889 and 1890, are in pamphlet form, and some of them are still in manuscript, thereby making it very inconvenient for the courts and all officers to intelligently understand the same, and in some cases the officers are not supplied with the above said laws.

Therefore be it resolved by the General Council of the Choctaw Nation assembled, that the sum of two thousand and five hundred dollars ($2,500) be and is hereby appropriated out of any money in the National Treasury not otherwise appropriated, and the same be placed in the hands of the Principal Chief, C. N., and the said Principal Chief is hereby authorized and empowered to employ two competent men whose duty it shall be to collect and translate into the Choctaw language all the laws above named and have them bound in good substantial binding book form, two hundred and fifty books of each, the Choctaw and English languages, and the Principal Chief is hereby authorized to pay to said two men employed by him as above provided so soon as they are ready to commence the work, the sum of one thousand dollars so as to enable them to purchase material, etc., for the said work, and the Chief shall pay balance, one thousand five hundred ($1,500) when the work is completed and turned over to him to be distributed to the several officers of this Nation. And the National Secretary is hereby directed and requested to furnish certified copies of all laws of the above said dates to the men so employed by the Principal Chief when they shall demand the laws.

And this resolution take effect and be in force from and after its passage.

Approved Oct. 31, 1890.

W. N. JONES, P. C. C. N.

NO. 24.

A resolution accepting the report of Dr. A. Griffith, Superintendent of New Hope Seminary, C. N.

To the General Council:

Your committee on schools, to whom was referred the report of A. Griffith, Superintendent of New Hope Seminary, find the same to be true and correct, with the balance on hand amounting to $764.92, and ask the passage of the following resolution, to-wit:

SEC. 1. Be it resolved by the General Council of the Choctaw Nation assembled, that the report of Dr. A. Griffith, Superintendent of New Hope Seminary, be and the same is hereby accepted as being true and correct, and that this resolution shall take effect and be in force from and after its passage.

Approved Oct. 31, 1890.

W. N. JONES, P. C. C. N.

NO. 25.

An act conferring citizenship on Mrs. Trehern, and other Mississippi Choctaws.

Be it enacted by the General Council of the Choctaw Nation assembled, that Mrs. Trehern and her children, Joel Trehern, Joseph Trehern, Laura (Trehern) Walker, her husband, Sam Walker and two children, Hannah (Trehern) Deloach, her husband, Joseph Deloach and their three children, all late of the State of Mississippi, be and are hereby recognized as citizens of the Choctaw Nation and entitled to all the rights, privileges and immunities of citizens of this Nation, and this act take effect and be in force from and after its passage.

Approved Oct. 31, 1890.

W. N. JONES, P. C. C. N.

NO. 26.

An act to punish official corruption, and the bribery of voters.

Be it enacted by the General Council of the Choctaw Nation assembled.

SEC. 1. Any Choctaw citizen holding any office of honor, trust or profit, under the Choctaw Government, and any witness or juror in any Choctaw courts who shall corruptly take or accept any money, valuable thing or consideration whatever, either before or after such officer, witness or juror has qualified, offered him or her by any other person with intent to influence the official action or duty of such officer, witness or juror, shall be deemed guilty of a felony, and upon indictment and conviction thereof, shall be punished by a fine of not less than one hundred dollars, and in default of the payment of such fine for one day, shall receive not less than thirty-nine (39) nor more than one hundred (100) lashes well laid on the bare back.

SEC. 2. Any person who shall corruptly offer, or attempt to offer to any qualified voter of the Choctaw Nation at any general or special election held under the Choctaw laws, any intoxicating liquor, money or valuable thing whatever, as a consideration for the suffrage of said voter, or with intent to influence said voter, as to his vote, or to subvert his free choice, shall be deemed guilty of a felony, and upon indictment and conviction, shall be punished as provided in Sec. 1, of this act.

This act shall take effect from and after its passage and approval.

Approved Nov. 3, 1890.

W. N. JONES, P. C. C. N.

NO. 27.

An act to change the County court ground of Nashoba County.

Be it enacted by the General Council of the Choctaw Nation assembled, that the County Court ground of Nashoba county, now known as Shawa court ground, be and the same is hereby removed to a spring one and one-half miles west of the present site, and one-half mile south of Madison Jefferson's place, and shall still be called and known as Shawa court ground, and that this act shall take effect and be in force from and after its passage.

Approved Nov. 3, 1890.

W. N. JONES, P. C. C. N.

NO. 28.

An act granting a charter to Moses Woolridge.

Be it enacted by the General Council of the Choctaw Nation assembled, that the right is hereby given to Moses Woolridge to turnpike the road in San Bois county, known as the Fort Smith and Eufaula road, commencing where said road crosses Imachaya creek and extending west to the foot of Broken Hill, a distance of seventeen miles, and of establishing a toll gate thereon. But before the said Moses Woolridge shall collect toll on said road, he shall, by proper means, make the said road in every particular a first-class turnpike road, after which he shall be entitled to receive from all non-citizens passing over said road, tolls as follows: For every four wheeled wagon drawn by four or more animals, 50 cents; for every four wheeled wagon or other vehicle drawn by two animals, 25 cents; for all two wheel carts drawn by one animal, 10 cents; for every person on horse back, 5 cents; for every person on foot, 5 cents; for every animal in droves, 1 cent per head, and the right herein granted shall continue so long as the turnpike is kept in first-class condition and for ten years.

Be it further enacted, that any non-citizen passing over this turnpike and refusing or failing to comply with the charges of this charter, shall be reported to the Indian Agent, who shall take such steps as will be necessary in order to compel said non-citizen to comply with this act, and that this act take effect and be in force from and after its passage.

Approved Nov. 3, 1890.

W. N. JONES, P. C. C. N.

NO. 29.

An act making an appropriation of one thousand dollars for the benefit of New Hope Seminary.

Be it enacted by the General Council of the Choctaw Nation assembled, that the sum of one thousand dollars, or so much thereof as is necessary, is hereby appropriated out of any money in the National Treasury and placed in the hands of the Board of Education, to build a furnace with proper pipes to heat the main dormitory at New Hope Seminary. That the Board of Education is hereby empowered to carry out the intentions of this act and to return any balance on hand to the National Treasury, and this act shall take effect and be in force from and after its passage.

Approved Nov. 3, 1890.

W. N. JONES, P. C. C. N.

NO. 30.

An act appropriating $7,000 for the benefit of Armstroug Orphan School.

Be it enacted by the General Council of the Choctaw Nation assembled, that the sum of seven thousand dollars is hereby appropriated to erect a new building, and to repair the present one at Armstrong Orphan Academy.

Be it further enacted, that all of this appropriation, or so much as is necessary, shall be expended under the supervision and consent of the Board of Education, and any balance on hand shall be turned into the treasury by the President of the Board of Education.

SEC. 3. The sum of six thousand two hundred dollars is hereby appropriated to be expended in the same manner for the use and benefit of Spencer Academy. This act shall take effect from and after its passage.

Approved Nov. 3, 1890.

W. N. JONES, P. C. C. N.

NO. 31.

An act in reference to licensed traders.

Be it enacted by the General Council of the Choctaw Nation, assembled, that licensed traders shall pay annually the sum of five hundred dollars for the privilege of selling goods or trading in the Choctaw Nation; that this act shall apply to every non-citizen who trades or exposes goods for sale in any manner, and if a trader conduct a business at more than one point he shall pay the like sum of five hundred dollars for each and every such business.

SEC. 2. That all acts or parts of acts in conflict herewith are hereby repealed, and this act take effect and be in force from and after the first day of January, A. D. 1891.

Approved Nov. 4, 1890.

W. N. JONES, P. C. C. N.

NO. 32.

A Memorial.

Whereas, a corporation known as the Choctaw Coal and Railway Company, operating under a charter granted by the laws of the State of Minnesota, were granted a charter by the Congress of the United States in 1887, to construct and operate a railway, telegraph and telephone lines through the Indian Territory, from a point on Red River, known as Rocky Cliff, to a point contiguous to Polk or Sevier counties, Arkansas; and whereas, said corporation were granted a right of way of one hundred feet along the main line and branches of said railroad; and whereas, said railroad compay has fenced and are fencing a right of way along the line of said railway that is one hundred feet on each side of the main track, without authority of law, and contrary to treaty rights or charter privileges, and against the wishes and over the protest of the Choctaw people; and whereas, it is believed by the Choctaw Council that said corporation has violated its charter rights by endeavoring to obtain possession of more land land in the Choctaw Nation than is granted in their right of way; and whereas, said charter expressly declares that such action on the part of this corporation shall operate a forfeiture of its charter; and whereas, said corporation have aided, assisted and advised disloyal Choctaw citizens in a violation of Choctaw laws, as tends to change the present tenure of the Choctaw tribe of Indians in their lands; and whereas, said corporation erected a wire fence along their railroad, without putting on blind, as required by Choctaw law, and has erected such a fence as is forbidden by iaw.

Therefore be it resolved by the General Council of the Choctaw Nation, that Honorable Secretary of the Interior be and he is hereby respectfully requested to investigate the action of the said Choctaw Coal and Railway Company, and have the fences so erected by said corporation, which are hereby declared to be a nuisance, removed, and that he request the Congress of the United States to revoke the charter of said corporation.

Resolved further, that the National Secretary be and is hereby instracted to forward by registered package a receipt for which shall be filed in his office within thirty days from this date, to the Secretary of the Interior and the President of the United

States, a copy of this memorial, under the seal of the Choctaw Nation.

Resolved further, that the Secretary of Interior is hereby respectfully requested to give this matter his careful attention, that this complaint may be acted upon as soon as possible.

Approved Nov. 11, 1890.

W. N. JONES, P. C C. N.

NO. 33.

Whereas, the General Council of the Choctaw Nation did, in its session of 1887, Nov. 10, pass a resolution declaring one W. H. McKinney, at that time District Trustee of the 2nd District, Choctaw Nation, a defaulter to the Nation in the sum of two thousand one hundred and seventy-five dollars and sixty cents, and did pass a resolution authorizing and directing the District Attorney of the said 2d District to prosecute the said W. H. McKinney and his sureties on his bond for the recovery of the said sum of $2,175.60, and the said cause of prosecution is still pending; and whereas, the said W. H. McKinney was elected Superintendent of public schools of the Choctaw Nation; and whereas, it is evident that some of the members of the Council did not know of the existence of said prosecution when they voted for him.

Therefore be it resolved by the General Council of the Choctaw Nation assembled, that the Principal Chief is hereby requested to withhold the commission of the said W. H. McKinney until he make a settlement with the Nation for the said sum of $2,175.60, for which he is defaulter, and in the event the said W. H. McKinney refuse or fail to make a settlement for the said amount, the Principal Chief is hereby authorized to appoint some suitable person to fill the vacancy of Superintendent of public schools as the law directs, and this resolution take effect and be in force from and after its passage.

Approved Nov. 11, 1890.

W. N. JONES, P. C. C. N.

NO. 34.

An act to authorize D. W. Hodges to construct a Railroad switch or tramway, and granting the right of way, etc.

SEC. 1. Be it enacted by the General Council of the Choctaw Nation assembled, that D. W. Hodges is hereby authorized to construct a railroad switch or tramway, or either of which he may deem most practicable, from the Lehigh branch of the M. K. & T. railway, beginning at a point to be by him selected on said branch road, between Lehigh and Coal Gate, and running from thence in a northwesterly direction about six miles, to or within one mile of his coal mine or mines.

SEC. 2. Be it further enacted, that the right of way is hereby granted to said D. W. Hodges to construct such railroad switch or tramway, and the same shall extend for fifty feet on each side of the track and continue as long as the same shall be used for the purpose set forth in this act; and said right shall be the use and benefit of D. W. Hodges and his heirs and assigns so long as used for said purpose.

SEC. 3. Be it further enacted, that this act shall not be construed to require the completion of said track the full distance of this grant, but that a less distance may be completed if so desired by the said D. W. Hodges. The right herein granted shall not be construed to interfere with the right or claim of other citizens of this Nation.

Sec. 4. Be it further enacted, that the right herein granted, if transferred to non-citizens, shall cease; and that this act shall take effect and be in force from and after its passage.

Approved Nov. 11, 1890.

W. N. JONES, P. C. C. N.

NO. 35.

An act for the better securing the safety of the election returns in the election of Principal Chief and of the National officers.

Be it enacted by the General Council of the Choctaw Nation assembled,

SEC. 1. That at every election for Principal Chief, or for any or all of the National officers, upon the delivery by the Sheriff or his deputy, to the proper Supreme Judge of the poll books of such Sheriff's county, said Judge shall give to such Sheriff a receipt, naming each poll book received, and particularly describing the condition of the same, whether securely sealed, mutilated or not.

SEC. 2. The Supreme Judge shall at once deposit such poll books in a secure box or other safe receptacle, in which there shall be kept no other thing except the poll books containing the returns of election for Principal Chief, or for national officers. He shall retain said poll books in said box or receptacle, under lock and key, until such time as he is by law required to transmit them to the National Secretary. While said books are in his possession the Supreme Judge shall not exhibit the same to any one, nor permit any person, under any pretext to inspect or to handle them.

SEC. 3. At the proper time such Judge shall, in person, take said poll books to the National Secretary, who shall give to such Judge receipt in all respects similar to those required herein to be given by the Supreme Judge to the various Sheriffs.

SEC. 4. Upon the delivery by the National Secretary to the Speaker of the House of such poll books, said Speaker shall give similar receipts to said Secretary.

SEC. 5. It shall be the duty of each Supreme Judge to preserve duplicates, made at the time, of all receipts so given by him to the various Sheriffs. These duplicates he shall deliver to said Speaker of the House in person, as soon as practicable after he has delivered the poll books to the National Secretary.

SEC. 6. In case any Supreme Judge is unable by reason of sickness or other unavoidable casualty, to deliver the poll books and duplicate receipts in person to the National Secretary and Speaker of the House, respectively, as herein above required, then he shall at once notify the National Secretary of such inability. The National Secretary shall thereupon proceed in person to the place where such Supreme Judge may be, and then receive from him the poll books and duplicate receipts, and deliver to him receipts as herein above required, and the National Secretary shall then deliver the books and duplicate receipts to the Speaker, as aforesaid. In case of the inability of the National Secretary to act as provided in this section, then the President of the Senate shall designate some one of the National officers to act in his stead.

SEC. 7. And be it further enacted, that if any judge of election fail to certify to any poll books, or, after having certified thereto, refuse to deliver the same, in manner and form as prescribed by law, then, in either such event, he shall be deemed guilty of a felony and he shall, upon indictment and conviction thereof, be punished by a fine of not less than one hundred dollars ($100) nor more than five hundred dollars ($500), and in case he fails to pay the fine assessed within one day, he shall receive not less than thirty-nine (39) nor more than one hundred (100) lashes well laid on his bare back, and this act shall take effect and be in force from and after its passage.

Approved Nov. 13, 1890.

W. N. JONES, P. C. C. N.

NO. 36.

Resolution of Adjournment.

Be it resolved by the General Council of the Choctaw Nation assembled, that the session of the General Council will adjourn on Friday evening at 3 o'clock, the 14th of Nov. 1890.

This resolution shall take effect from and after its passage.

Approved Nov. 13, 1890.

W. N. JONES, P. C. C. N.

NO. 37.

An act establishing an additional election precinct in Jack's Fork County.

Be it enacted by the General Council of the Choctaw Nation assembled, that an additional precinct is hereby established at Antlers Station, in Jack's Fork county, and called and known as Antlers Precinct, and all the citizens of Jack's Fork are privileged to vote at said precinct in all special and general elections and that this act take effect and be in force from and after its passage.

Approved Nov. 13, 1890.

W. N. JONES, P. C. C. N.

NO. 38.

An act removing an election precinct in Wade County.

Be it enacted by the General Council of the Choctaw Nation assembled, that the election precinct heretofore established at Davis Anderson's house, in Wade county, and known as Davis Anderson precinct, be and the same is hereby moved to the school house in Pleasant Hill neighborhood, and shall be known as and called Pleasant Hill precinct, and the voters may vote at said precinct.

This act shall take effect and be in force from and after its passage.

Approved Nov. 13, 1890.

W. N. JONES, P. C. C. N.

NO. 39.

An act establishing an election precinct in Nashoba County.

Be it enacted by the General Council of the Choctaw Nation assembled, that an additional precinct is hereby established at Good Water, in Nashoba county, and shall be called Good Water precinct, and all the legal voters of Nashoba county are privileged to vote at said precinct in all special and general elections, and this act take effect and be in force from and after its passage.

Approved Nov. 13, 1890.

W. N. JONES, P. C. C. N.

NO. 40.

An act to facilitate the detection of larceny of cattle in the Choctaw Nation.

Be it enacted by the General Council of the Choctaw Nation assembled, that every butcher doing business in this Nation shall keep a written record of the marks and brands of all cattle and hogs purchased for slaughter and from whom purchased; at the end of each month he shall file the same with the Clerk of the County Court in the county in which such butcher does business.

SEC. 2. It shall be the duty of each County Clerk to safely preserve such record so filed and to freely permit the public to inspect the same.

SEC. 3. The violation of any of the provisions of this act shall constitute a misdemeanor, and shall be punished by a fine of not less than \$5 nor more than \$25. In case the offender be a non-citizen his license as butcher permit shall be revoked.

SEC. 4. This act shall take effect from and after its passage and approval.

Approved Nov. 13, 1890.

W. N. JONES, P. C. C. N.

NO. 41.

To the Senate and House of Representatives:

Your committee on Finance would most respectfully report unto your honorable bodies that George Oaks, Inspector for the south end of the St. Louis & San Francisco railroad, has failed to make any report, hence your committee are unable to ascertain the amount of his collection, nor has he made any report to the National Treasurer.

Therefore be it resolved by the General Council of the Choctaw Nation assembled, that the Principal Chief be and he is hereby directed to cause proper steps to be taken to compel him to make proper report, and to recover immediately all moneys collected by him, and pay the same over to the National Treasurer, and this resolution be in force from and after its passage.

Approved Nov. 14, 1890.

W. N. JONES, P. C. C. N.

NO. 42.

A resolution authorizing Principal Chief of the Choctaw Nation to make appointments, etc.

Be it resolved by the General Council of the Choctaw Nation assembled, that the Principal Chief of the Choctaw Nation is hereby authorized to appoint one or more competent person or persons to investigate W. J. B. Lloyd's account, a former Superintendent of Armstrong Academy, and make a final settlement with the said W. J. B. Lloyd, and make his or their report to next General Council, and this resolution shall take effect and be in force from and after its passage.

Approved Nov. 14, 1890.

W. N. JONES, P. C. C. N.

NO. 43.

An act recognizing the citizenship of Willis Jackson and his family.

Be it enacted by the General Council of the Choctaw Nation assembled; that Willis Jackson, his wife, Mary Jackson and their children, Minnie, Sam, Folsom, Laura and Edmond Jackson, late of the State of Mississippi, are hereby recognized and declared to be citizens of this Nation, and entitled to all the rights, privileges and immunities of other citizens of this Nation, and this act shall take effect and be in force from and after its passage.

Approved Nov. 13, 1890.

W. N. JONES, P. C. C. N.

NO. 44.

An act making appropriation for the relief of Matt Sakki et als.

Be it enacted by the General Council of the Choctaw Nation assembled, that the sum of seventy-five dollars is hereby appropriated out of any money in the Treasury not otherwise appropriated, for the purpose of aiding Matt Sakki, Isaac Simsin and Tom Yark, lately arrived from Mississippi, and to enable them to pay their board and traveling expenses while attending the General Council for the purpose of having themselves recognized as citizens of this Nation, and this act shall take effect and be in force from and after its passage.

Approved Nov. 14, 1890.

W. N. JONES, P. C. C. N.

NO. 45.

An act changing the County Court ground of Scullyville County.

Be it enacted by the General Council of the Choctaw Nation assembled, that the county court ground of Scullyville is hereby removed from what is known as Scullyville court ground to a place at or near the crossing of Buck Creek, on the Fort Smith and Stringtown road, and it shall be called and known as Buck Creek court ground. The county court of Scullyville county shall hold its first session at Buck Creek court ground on the first Monday in February, 1891, and this act take effect and be in force from and after its passage.

Approved Nov. 14, 1890.

W. N. JONES, P. C. C. N.

NO. 46.

An act making appropriation for the fiscal year, ending July 31, 1891.

Be it enacted by the General Council of the Choctaw Nation assembled, that the following sums of money are hereby appropriated as follows:

Principal Chief	$ 2,000 00
Trea. Aud. & Sec.	1,800 00
National Agent	800 00
National Attorney	400 00
Private Secretary	500 00
National Lighthorse	950 00
Supreme Judges	1,200 00
Circuit Judges	1,500 00
County Judges	5,950 00
District Chief	150 00
District Attorneys	950 00
Election Clerks	260 00
Grand and petit jurors	14,900 00
Witness fees for Circuit court	6,000 00
Sup. of schools and Dist. Trustees	1,800 00
Local Trustees	1,500 00
Contingent fund for Chief	400 00
Contingent fund for Superintendent	450 00
Contingent fund for Dist. Trustees	225 00
Contingent fund for Auditor	400 00

Clk. Sup. Court	$ 100 00
Clk. Co. Court	1,700 00
Clk. Circuit Court	900 00
Sheriffs	5,950 00
Rangers	850 00
Sheriffs & duputies attending court	1,800 00
Deputy Sheriffs	7,400 00
Sheriff attending Sup. court	50 00
Election Judges	375 09
Contingent fund for Treasurer	400 00
Contingent fund for Secretary	50 00
Publication for Sec.	350 00
Care of Capitol one year	50 00
General Council	9,160 00
Light Horse attending Council	895 00
Clerk Citizenship Committee	155 00
Students in States 16 boys	4,700 00
Students in States 16 girls	4,300 00

NEIGHBORHOOD SCHOOLS.

1st District	$18,090 00	New Hope Sem.	$10,000 00
2d District	18,540 00	Armstrong Acad.	5,500 00
3d District	22,860 00	Wheelock Sem.	5,500 00
Spencer Academy	10,000 00		

SPECIAL APPROPRIATIONS.

Repairing Armstrong Academy	$7,000 00	Prosecution Choctaw Coal & R'y Co.	$2,000 00
Repairing Spencer Academy	6,000 00	Publication & translation of laws	2,500 00
Repairing New Hope Seminary	1,000 00	Pay of Ed Spring	89 65
		New female sem.	20,000 00
		New male academy	20,000 00

And this act shall take effect and be in force from and after its passage.

Approved Nov. 14, 1890.

W. N. JONES, P. C. C. N.

NO. 48.

An act to defray expenses of committee attending funeral of Ex-Governor Edmond McCurtain.

Be it enacted by the General Council of the Choctaw Nation assembled, that the sum of one hundred and forty-seven dollars and fifty cents is hereby appropriated out of any money in the National Treasury not otherwise appropriated, to defray the actual traveling expenses of committee appointed by the General Council to attend the funeral of Ex-Governor Edmond McCurtain, and upon presentation of Auditor's warrant, the Treasurer shall pay the same.

SEC. 2. That this take effect and be in force from and after its passage.

Approved Nov. 14, 1890.

W. N. JONES, P. C. C. N.

NO. 49.

To the General Council of the Choctaw Nation assembled:

We, your committee to whom was referred the report of Green McCurtain, National Treasurer, would respectfully report as follows. We find that the Treasurer has received revenues as followes, viz :

From the general government	$61,362 63	Chicago, Kan. & Nebraska	$ 269 21
Atoka Coal & Mining Co Aug '90	20,493 28	Choctaw Coal & R'y Co.	750 00
Osage Coal & Mining Co July '90	22,551 01	St. L. & S. F. R'y gravel	56 44
S. W. Coal & Improvement Comp'y Aug '90	13,518 75	S. F. Holsm	110 90
		C. C. R'y Co. Mining	1,276 45
Collector, 1st District, 1890	6,763 52	Total	$153,267 76
Collector, 2d District, 1889	522 36	To which add amount recd. from W. N. Jones former treasurer	$111,091 64
Collector, 3d District, 1889			
Inspector, North Frisco	2,075 56	Bal. net proceed fund from R. L. Owen	22,438 47
Inspector, South end, 1889	663 00		
Inspector D. & W. V. R. R.	112 72		
Inspector C. C. & R'y Co.	16,226 04	Making a grand total of	$286,797 87
Inspector M. K. & T. R'y	2,933 89	Less warants pd by Treasurer during year ending Oct 1, 1890	$144,242 95
Frisco right of way	2,250 00		
Kansas & Valley right of way	57 37		
Gulf, Colorado & Santa Fe	1,125 00	Leaving balance on hand for acct. current	$142,554 92
Southern Kan.	149 63		

We find further, that the amounts that coal companies pay to Treasurer do not exactly agree with the weigher's reports. Sometimes companies pay more than weighers and sometimes less, but striking a general average the total amounts agree within a few dollars, so it is not necessary to institute an investigation, and would recommend that the following resolution be passed:

Be it resolved by the General Council of the Choctaw Nation assembled, that the report of Green McCartain, National Treasurer, for the year ending Oct. 1, 1890, showing a balance on hand of $142,554.92, be accepted as true and correct, and this resolution take effect and be in force from and after its passage.

Approved Nov. 14, 1890.

W. N. JONES, P. C. C. N.

NO. 50.

A resolution in reference to Dr. R. W. Hill's report.

Your committee on schools, to whom was referred the report of different schools, academies and seminaries, find them all to be true and correct, except Dr. R. W. Hill's report. We find a discrepancy against the Nation in the sum of $300, and ask the passage of the following resolution, to-wit:

Be it resolved by the General Council of the Choctaw Nation assembled, that the Superintendent of the National schools is hereby authorized to make a complete examination of the same in the presence of the said Dr. R. W. Hill, and make his report to the next General Council, and that this resolution shall take effect and be in force from and after its passage.

Approved Nov. 14, 1890.

W. N. JONES, P. C. C. N.

NO. 51.

To the Senate and House of Representatives:

Your committee to whom was referred the report of T. E. Oaks, District Collector for the 3d District, Choctaw Nation, find he collected for the fiscal year ending July, 31, 1890, ($7,209.18) seven thousand two hundred and nine dollars and eighteen cents, for which he has properly accounted to the National Treasurer.

Therefore be it resolved by the General Council of the Choctaw Nation assembled, that the report of T. E. Oaks, District

Collector for the 3d District, Choctaw Nation, be accepted as true and correct, and this resolution be in force from and after its passage.

Approved Nov. 14, 1890.

W. N. JONES, P. C. C. N.

NO. 52.

A resolution in reference to A Docking, Superintendent Spencer Academy.

Whereas, a resolution, No. 57, passed and approved last General Council, charging A. Docking as being a discrepancy against the Nation the sume of $372. The report was made by Dr. R. W. Hill, who was acting Superintendent at that time, and not A Docking, as was stated in the said resolution No. 57. He is innocent as to the charges preferred against him; therefore we ask the passage of the following resolution, to-wit:

Be it resolved by the General Council of the Choctaw Nation assembled, that the charges preferred against the said A. Docking as being a discrepancy against the Nation of $372, in the said resolution No. 57, is hereby repealed, and that this resolution shall take effect and be in force from and after its passage.

Approved Nov. 14, 1890.

W. N. JONES, P. C. C. N.

NO. 53.

To the General Council of the Choctaw Nation assembled:

Your committee to whom was referred the report of L. G. Folsom, Collector for the 2d District, Choctaw Nation, find that he collected from all sources the sum of $330.56 up to Jan. 31, 1890. and makes no report for the balance of the year, and he has not paid any of the collections over to the Treasurer, as the law requires and is culpably negligent under the law.

Therefore be it resolved by the General Council of the Choctaw Nation assembled, that the principal Chief be hereby authorized to take the necessary steps to cause said L. G. Folsom to make final and satisfactory settlement with the Treasurer, and this resolution be in full force and effect from and after its passage.

Approved Nov. 14, 1890.

W. N. JONES, P. C. C. N.

NO. 54.

Whereas, a corporation known as the Choctaw Coal and Railway Company, incorporated under the laws of the State of Minnesota, and chartered by the Congress of the United States, to establish a certain line of railway through the Choctaw Nation with branch roads, and

Whereas, by the terms of their charter they are allowed a branch road in a westerly direction to their coal fields in Tobucksy county, and

Whereas they are building numerous branches or switches, and are contemplating the building of a road in a southerly direction from or near Hartshorn, a station on said branch road, to Denison, or Bonham, Texas, and

Whereas, certain officials of said Choctaw Coal and Railway Company are said to be engaged in speculating in town sites under illegal leases from Choctaw citizens, and are erecting houses, offices, etc., on said leased lands and are renting them, and

Whereas, said leases of land are in direct violatson of law, and

Whereas, no contract is recognized for coal or stone for a longer period than six years, and

Whereas, certain citizens have leased said coal for a term of years (viz: 30) not recognized by law.

Sec. 1. Therefore be it enacted by the General Council of the Choctaw Nation assembled, that the Choctaw Council hereby enters a protest against the building of said branch road from Hartshorn south.

Sec. 2. Be it further enacted, that the National Agent is hereby instructed to demand of the officials of the Choctaw Coal and Railway Company that they file within sixty days, evidence that they are not connected directly or indirectly with the town site syndicates; also a copy shall be filed with the principal Chief. If they fail to file such evidence the National Agent shall declare their coal contracts null and void and so notify them.

Sec. 3. Be it further enacted, that the leases for thirty years are hereby declared to be illegal and null and void.

Sec. 4. Be it further enacted, that the Sheriff of each county is hereby instructed to at once diligently inquire into all such illegal leases and report the same to the principal Cheif, and that the cause any improvement erected by non-citizens, corporate or individual, by virtue of said illegal leases, to be advertised for sale in the manner provided by law.

SEC. 5. Be it further enacted, that the principal Chief is hereby authorized to employ competent counsel to represent the interest of the Nation before the United States courts, and the sum of $2,000 is hereby appropriated out of any money in the Treasury not otherwise appropriated, for the payment of said attorneys. Said amount to be drawn by the principal Chief on his own certificate and disbursed as to him seems best and the remainder, if any, to be paid into the National Treasury. All records in such cases to be filed in the office of the National Secretary.

SEC. 6. Be it furthur enacted, that a copy of this act be forwarded to the President and Treasurer of said Choctaw Coal and Railway Company by the National Secretary, and that this act shall take effect and be in force from and after its passage.

Approved Nov. 14, 1890.

W. N. JONES, P. C. C. N.

This is to certify that the foregoing is a true and correct copy of the acts of the General Council of the Choctaw Nation, passed and approved at the October term thereof, 1890.

{ L.S. } Witness my hand and the great seal of the Choctaw Nation, this the 12th day of December, A. D. 1890.

J. B. JACKSON,

National Secretary, Choctaw Nation.

LAWS

OF THE

CHOCTAW NATION

MADE AND ENACTED BY THE.

GENERAL COUNCIL,

FROM

1886 TO 1890 INCLUSIVE.

1890.
INDIAN CITIZEN PRINT,
ATOKA, I. T.

INDEX.

LAWS OF THE
CHOCTAW NATION,

FROM 1886 TO 1890 INCLUSIVE.

———o———

BILL I.

An Act to increase the salary of the Superintendent of Public Schools.

Be it enacted by the General Council of the Choctaw Nation assembled, That the act providing the salary of the Superintendent of Public Schools is hereby amended and changed so that said salary shall be Four Hundred Dollars per annum, and this Act shall take effect and be in force from and after its passage.

APPROVED, This 12th day of October, 1886.

T. McKINNEY,
P. C. C. N.

BILL II.

An Act to prohibit the sale or manufacture of Choctaw Beer, cider or any other kind of malt, fermented, distilled or any other kind of intoxicating liquor, or beverage.

Be it enacted by the General Council of the Choctaw Nation assembled, That the sale or manufacture of Choctaw Beer,

Cider or any kind of malt, fermented or Distilled Liquors or beverage or intoxicant of any kind whatsoever in the Choctaw Nation is hereby prohibited and the same authority is given to the officers to suppress it and the same pains and penalties to violators of this law as if they were engaged in the sale or manufacture of whisky and this Act shall take effect and be in force from and after its passage.

APPROVED, October 18, 1886.

T. McKINNEY,
P. C. C. N.

BILL III.

An Act establishing Jackson County.

Be it enacted by the General Council of the Choctaw Nation assembled, That a County to be called Jackson County is hereby created out of a portion Kiamitia, Blue and Atoka Counties. The following shall be the boundary lines of said County to wit:

Beginning at the mouth of Boggy; thence up Boggy to the forks of Muddy and Clear Boggies; thence up Muddy Boggy to the Thompson Wesley Ford; thence by the Old Atoka place at the edge of the bottom then on the new blazed road to Hettie Carne's on Clear Boggy; thence down the Caddo road to Wilson Jone's pasture; thence along the eastern string of said pasture to the Old Boggy Depot road; thence down said road to Jack Risner's leaving Jack Risner's place 250 yards within the limits of Jackson County, thence down the Phelin Wahle Branch to Blue River; thence down Blue River to Red River; thence down Red River to the mouth of Boggy, the beginning.

APPROVED, October 21, 1886.

T. McKINNEY,
P. C. C. N.

BILL IV.

An Act to appoint two additional Inspectors.

Be it enacted by the General Council of the Choctaw Nation assembled, That the Principal Chief is hereby authorized to appoint two additional Inspectors to operate on the St. Louis and San Francisco Rail Road. One Inspector to work from Ft. Smith, Arkansas to Tushka Homma, C. N. and from Tuska Homma C. N., to Red River, C. N. Said Inspectors to be Citizens of the Choctaw Nation.

SEC. 2. Be it further enacted that the said Inspector shall be appointed in accordance with the law passed and approved at the October 1883 session of the General Council.

SEC. 3. Be it further enacted, That the office of Inspector provided for in the Act of November 6, 1883, be confined to the M., K. & T. Rail Road and its branches in the Choctaw Nation, And this Act take effect and be in force from and after its passage.

APPROVED, October, 22, 1886.

THOMPSON McKINNEY,
P. C. C. N.

BILL V.

An Act giving Jackson County one Representative.

Be it enacted by the General Council of the Choctaw Nation assembled, That hereafter Jackson County shall be entitled to one Representative to be elected by the qualified voters of said County, and that this Act take effect and be in force from and after its passage.

APPROVED, October 29, 1886.

T. McKINNEY.
P. C. C. N.

BILL VI.

An Act creating a Senatorial District in Pushmataha District.

Be it enacted by the General Council of the Choctaw Nation assembled, That from and after the passage of this Act the Counties of Blue and Jackson shall compose one Senatorial District and they shall be entitled to one Senator in the General Council.

Be it further enacted, That this Act take effect and be in force from and after August 1st 1886.

APPROVED, October 29, 1886.

T. McKINNEY.
P. C. C. N.

BILL VII.

A Resolution respecting suits now pending in the 3rd District.

Be it enacted by the General Council of the Choctaw Nation assembled, That all suits of whatever nature now pending in the County Courts of Blue, Atoka and Kiamitia Counties wherein the Plaintiff and Defendant are both residents of Jackson County, and shall be transferred to the County Court of Jackson County, and it is hereby made the duty of the Judge of Jackson County when organized to demand and receipt for, of the respective clerks of the Counties above named, all the papers in said suits, but if both plaintiff and defendant are not residents of Jackson County, then the suits to remain for adjudication in the Courts where they were brought and that this resolution take effect and be in force from and after February 1, 1886.

APPROVED, October 29, 1886.

THOMPSON McKINEY,
P. C. C. N.

BILL VIII.

An Act amending an Act relative to Deputy Sheriffs.

Be it enacted by the General Council of the Choctaw Nation assembled, That Blue County shall be entitled to four Deputy Sheriffs and the Counties of Atoka, Kiamitia, Jacksfork and Jackson shall each be entitled to four Deputy Sheriffs and all Deputies appointed under this Act and no more shall be allowed a salary of Fifty Dollars to be paid out of the National Treasury on the certificate of the Principal Sheriffs, and that this Act take effect and be in force from and after February 1, 1887.

APPROVED, October 30, 1886.

THOMPSON McKINNEY,
P. C. C. N.

BILL IX.

An Act amending an Act relative to jurors in 3rd Judicial District.

Be it enacted by the General Council of the Choctaw Nation assembled, That the Jury of the Circuit Court in the 3rd District at the August term, thereof 1887 and at each succeeding shall be selected as follows to wit: Blue County shall have eight Jurors, Atoka County shall have eight Jurors, Jacksfork County shall have eight Jurors, Kiamitia County and Jackson County shall have eight Jurors, and be it further enacted that all Acts or parts of Acts heretofore passed coming in any manner in conflict with this Act, be and the same is hereby repealed and that this Act take effect and be in force from and after March 1, 1887.

APPROVED, October 30, 1886.

THOMPSON McKINNEY,
P. C. C. N.

BILL X.

An Act entitled an Act changing the Circuit Court, Pushmataha District, Choctaw Nation from Atoka County to Jackson County, Choctaw Nation.

Be it enacted by the General Council of the Choctaw Nation assembled, That the Circuit Court of Pushmataha District is hereby removed from Tiak Hili in Atoka County, to Tiak Hili in Jackson County, C. N., and the February 1887 term and all future terms of the Circuit Court of Pushmataha District shall be held at Tiak Hili in Jackson County, C. N. and this Act be in force from and after its passage.

APPROVED, November 1, 1886.

THOMPSON McKINNEY,
P. C. C. N.

BILL XI.

An Act authorizing the Sheriff of Jackson County to act as Sheriff of the Circuit Court in Pushmataha District.

Be it enacted by the General Council of the Choctaw Nation assembled, That the Sheriff of Jackson County is hereby empowered and authorized to Act as Sheriff of the Circuit Court in Pushmataha District to serve and execute all legal process that may eminate from said court and demand, receive and receipt from the former Sheriff of said court all papers and process for execution that may be in his hands, and all laws coming in any manner in conflict with the provisions of this Act is hereby repealed, and that this Act take effect and be in force from and after February 1, 1887.

APPROVED, November 1, 1886.

THOMPSON McKINNEY,
P. C. C. N.

BILL XII.

An Act entitled an Act defining the quantity of blood necessary for citizenship.

SECTION, 1. Be it enacted by the General Council of the Choctaw Nation assembled, That hereafter all persons non-citizens of the Choctaw Nation making,or presenting to the General Council,petitions for rights of Choctaws in this Nation shall be required to have one eighth Choctaw blood and shall be required to prove the same by competent Testimony.

SEC. 2. Be it enacted that all applicants for rights in this Nation shall prove their mixture of blood to be white and Indian.

SEC. 3. Be it further enacted that no persons convicted of

any felony or high crime shall be admitted to rights of citizenship within this Nation.

SEC. 4. Be it further enacted that this Act shall not be construed to effect persons within the limits of the Choctaw Nation now enjoying the rights of Citizenship.

SEC. 5. Be it further enacted that this Act take effect and be in force from and after its passage.

BILL XIII.

An Act allowing the Ranger a salary of Fifty Dollars.

Be it enacted by the General Council of the Choctaw Nation assembled, That the several Rangers of the Counties of this Nation in addition to the fees already allowed them by law, be paid the sum of fifty dollars out of the National Treasury, on the certificate of the County Clerk, said salary to be paid quarterly, and this Act take effect and be in force from and after its passage.

APPROVED, November 5, 1886.

THOMPSON McKINNEY,
P. C. C. N.

BILL XIV.

SECTION 1. Be it enacted by the General Council of the Choctaw Nation assembled, That it shall not be lawful for any non-citizen of this Nation, whether under a traders permit, or any other permit to reside or do business in the Nation to enclose for his own use and benefit any more lands than sufficient to build a tenement or business house upon, and if a merchant to build a business house not to exceed in a town or village more than two town lots of usual size.

SEC. 2. Non-citizens who own houses and buildings for the purpose of renting them, and are renting them, shall within sixty days from the passage of this Act dispose of same, or be dealt with in the same manner as provided for in the sale of non-citizens improvments the law of October 30, 1887 in reference thereto.

SEC. 3. All enclosures or pastures owned by non-citizens shall be sold to Citizens within sixty days from passage of this Act, or they shall be removed by the Sheriff of the County where said enclosure or pasture are located or opened up for common pasture purpose to the citizens of the Nation.

SEC. 4. Non-citizens failing or refusing to comply with the requirements of the 1st Section of this Act shall be deemed and held as forfeiting their permits and shall be further held to be intruders and their removal shall be demanded by the Principal Chief, and this Act take effect and be in force from and after its passage.

APPROVED, October 28, 1887.

THOMPSON McKINNEY,
P. C. C. N.

BILL XV.

An Act to define the duties of the Officers of the Choctaw Nation who deal with intruders.

Be it enacted by the General Council of the Choctaw Nation assembled, That it shall be the duty of the Sheriff to deal with intruders and non-citizens; to make a sworn statement before any Judge of this Nation; to the principal Chief in every case of refusal to take out a permit, or failing to get the necessary signers to his petition or refusal to leave the Nation when notified by the Sheriff or any other Officer, authorized by law to deal with intruders and non-citizens, and it shall be the duty of the Principal Chief to forthwith report all intruders to the United States Indian Agent, when reported to him in accordance with this Act, and ask their removal.

SEC. 2. If any Sheriff shall fail, neglect or refuse to carry out this Act, he shall be deemed and held to be guilty of a misdemeanor, and shall be prosecuted against, to the Circuit Court and shall be fined not less than fifty dollars nor more than one hundred dollars in every case of failure, neglect, or refusal and this Act take effect and be in force from and after its passage.

APPROVED, November 14, 1887.

THOMPSON McKINNEY,
P. C. C. N.

BILL XVI.

An Act defining the duties of the National Auditor.

SEC. 1. Be it enacted by the General Council of the Choctaw Nation assembled, That it shall not be lawful for the National Auditor to issue a warrant on the National Treasury in any manner other than hereinafter provided.

SEC. 2. Be it further enacted, That it shall be the duty of the Auditor on and during the first part of the month of every succeeding quarter to make out a warrant in favor of every officer in this Nation, whose salary is payable by law out of the National Treasury for the amount that is due him as his salary for that quarter. The Auditor shall forward the warrants in favor of the National and District Officers direct to such officers. The salaries of all other officers shall be forwarded to the County Judge of each County, who shall deliver them to each officer for the purpose of this Act. It shall be the duty of the National Secretary to file with the National Auditor a list of the dates and duration of every commission issued by him.

The Sheriff of the Circuit Courts shall send to the Auditor the names and dates of appointment of his regular Deputies.

SEC. 3. Be it further enacted, That every officer in this Nation who collects or superintends the collection of public monies, shall make a report at the end of each month to the National Auditor of the amount of such collection; how, and on what they are made. On the basis of such reports the Auditor shall issue his warrant in favor of the officer for the amount that is due him.

SEC. 4. Be it further enacted, That all expenses of the Courts of this Nation payable by law, and out of the National Treasury, shall be by allowance of the Judge, and under the hand and seal of the Clerk. A certified list of all such expenses and the date of the law under which they are paid, shall be forwarded by the Clerk within one day after adjournment of each Court to the National Auditor.

SEC. 5. Be it further enacted, That this Act take effect and be in force from and after February 1, 1888.

APPROVED, Nov. 7, 1887.

T. McKINNEY, P. C. C. N.

BILL XVII.

Supplementary to an Act in relation to wire fences.

PASTURES.

Be it enacted by the General Council of the Choctaw Nation assembled, That no person or citizen shall be allowed to connect his pasture with that of another. There shall be a passage way or lane left between all of such enclosures not less than twenty-five feet wide. In all cases of violations of this Act the County Judge is hereby authorized to have such fences cut down by the Sheriff and the passage way kept clear, and this Act to take effect and be in force from and after its passage.

APPROVED, Nov. 8th, 1887.

T. McKINNEY,
P. C. C. N.

BILL XVIII.

An Act defining the manner of trying impeachment cases.

SEC. 1. Be it enacted by the General Council of the Choctaw Nation assembled, That any three citizens of the Choctaw Nation may, at any time, present charges to the Principal Chief against any National or District Officer of the Choctaw Nation, except himself, for any misdemeanor in office, and they may also in the same manner, and for the same reasons prefer charges against the Principal Chief to the General Council and file the same with the National Secretary.

SEC. 2. Said charges must be sworn to before some Judge of this Nation, and must be accompanied with full specification of the misdemeanor charged, and must be supported by at least two respectable witnesses and the Principal Chief is hereby authorized to administer all oaths necessary to the discharge of the trust imposed upon him by this Act.

SEC. 3. If in the judgement of the Principal Chief, said charges are of such a nature as to endanger the public good by allowing the officer against whom such are made to continue in the exercise of his office, he shall notify such officer to appear before him at some place and time, giving at least ten day's no–

tice, and show cause, if any he can, why he should not be suspended from exercising the duties of his office. In case said officer should fail to appear without giving a lawful excuse, the Principal Chief shall proceed with the examination the same as if said officer was present. After the Principal Chief has heard all of the evidence on both sides, if he is of the opinion that such officer should not exercise the duties of his office he shall suspend him from office. But in no case shall the Principal Chief suspend any officer except in pursuance of law.

. SEC. 4.—In all cases arising hereunder, the Principal Chief shall forward to the National Secretary, the charges, specifications, evidence, and his disposition of the case, who shall deliver all such papers to the speaker of the House of Representatives at the next ensuing Session of the General Council.

SEC. 5. When the House of Representatives is satisfied that there is good cause to impeach an officer, they shall make an article of impeachment against such officer and transmit the same to the Senate, and the House shall proceed, as soon as practicable, to elect managers to conduct the impeachment trial, and appoint a day for the appearance of the accused, and cause summons to be issued for him, signed by the President of the Senate and Countersigned by the Secretary, with a copy of the articles of impeachment annexed, requiring the accused to appear on the day appointed for the purpose, and be ready to answer the charges preferred against him. Said summons shall be served on the accused personally if he can be found, but if not, then by leaving a copy of the summons and articles of impeachment at the residence of the accused with some person over sixteen years old.

SEC. 6. For the purpose of this act the Sergeant-at-Arms, with such number of Deputies as may be certified to be necessary by the President of the Senate, shall execute all process of the Court of impeachment; provided, however, that said Deputies may be relieved at the discretion of such President, who is sitting as a court of impeachment. The Senate shall exercise all powers nescessary to a full jurisdiction, and final determination of the case before them, but if the accused fails to appear, after being notified, or after appearing fails to answer, the Senate may proceed EX PARTE.

SEC. 7. Before proceeding with the trial, the President of the Senate shall administer to all of its members, and the Secretary to the President, an oath to try and determine the charges and specification, and to do justice according to law and evidence and all being sworn the Senate shall proceed to hear, try and determine. Any case of impeachment may adjourn a trial to any other time, consulting the public good, and shall be the Sole Judge of all questions of law arising during the trial, the advisability of testimony, the competency of witnesses and any other question incident to its jurisdiction; and exercise all needful authority to enforce order and respect in as full a manner as a regular court of law could do, provided however that all votes given on any question whatever shall be VIVA VOCE, and entered on the minutes of said court of impeachment.

SEC. 8. Whenever articles of impeachment are pending against the principal chief, he shall be disqualified from holding the office, and the Chief or other Justice of the Supreme Court shall preside.

SEC. 9. The Secretary of the Senate shall make out a certified transcript of the proceedings had on any impeachment trial, and deposit the same in the office of National Secretary for future reference, and this act shall take effect and be in force from and after its passage.

APPROVED, November 8, 1887.

T. McKINNEY,
P. C. C. N.

BILL NO. XIX.

An act entitled an act prohibiting a citizen or citizens to employ non-citizens to take charge of stock of any kind as herdsmen.

Be it enacted by the General Council of the Choctaw Nation assembled, That it shall not be lawful for any citizen or citizens of this Nation to employ a non-citizen or non-citizens to take charge of his or her cattle, horses, mules, sheep, goats or hogs, or stock of any kind, and to hunt or gather stock of any kind running on the range within the limits of this nation, under consideration that this act is not to be construed to prevent citizens from employing non-citizens to take charge of stock, to feed in pen or pasture; and any person or persons charged with the violation of this act shall, upon conviction in the Circuit Court having jurisdiction, be fined in a sum not less than two hundred and fifty dollars nor more than five hundred dollars, in the discretion of the court, one-half of which fine shall go to the national treasury for national purposes, and the other half to the informant. Be it further enacted that any act or part of any act in anywise coming in conflict with the provisions of this act is hereby repealed, and this act shall take effect and be in force from and after its passage.

Passed over veto of Principal Chief November 9, 1887.

BILL NO. XX.

An act to provide for the security of the National Treasurer.

SEC. 1. Be it enacted by the General Council of the Choctaw Nation assembled, That the sum of four hundred dollars is hereby annually appropriated as a contingent fund for the use of the National Treasurer, to defray the contingent expenses of the office, and to pay the board and lodging of the Light Horse when acting as a body guard for the National Treasurer; provided the National Treasurer shall make a detailed statement annually to the General Council of his expenditure of the fund herein provided. For the purpose of this act the Principal Chief shall immediately on the passage appoint, on the recommendation of the National Treasurer, two Light Horsemen to be subject to the order of said Treasurer, and shall revoke the commission of the two Light Horse now on the force, unless the said Treasurer should recommend them, or either of them, and this act shall take effect and be in force from and after its passage.

APPROVED, November 9, 1887.

THOMPSON McKINNEY,
P. C. C. N.

BILL NO. XXI.

An act construing the treaty of 1866, in reference to missionaries.

Be it enacted by the General Council of Choctaw Nation assembled, That the scheme of changing the tenure of lands by the Choctaws and Chickasaws, as inaugurated by the eleventh article of the treaty of 1866, having failed, all of the conditions and contingencies connected with and dependent upon the change also failed; that all of those published articles of said treaty contemplating such a change are void, and missionaries, or any other class of persons mentioned therein, have no rights thereunder, and this act shall take effect and be in force from and after its passage.

APPROVED, November 9, 1887.

T. McKINNEY,
P. C. C. N.

BILL NO. XXII.

An act amendatory of the law of November 1, 1882, in reference to wild or prairie hay.

Be it enacted by the General Council of the Choctaw Nation assembled, That all that part of the law of November 1, 1882, which allows non-citizens or persons under legal permit, to cut, ship and sell prairie or wild grass fromthe common or public domain of this nation, is hereby repealed, and it is hereby further provided that non-citizens or persons under legal permit shall only obtain what prairie or wild grass or hay they want from citizens, and then only what is necessary for their own use. All violations of this act will subject the offenders to removal from the Nation, and this act shall take effect and be in force from and after its passage.

APPROVED, November 10, 1887.

THOMPSON McKINNEY,
P. C. C. N.

BILL NO. XXIII.

An act for the protection of the public buildings.

Be it enacted by the General Council of the Choctaw Nation assembled, That any person who shall deface, injure or destroy any public building of this Nation, shall, for each offense, be indicted by the Grand Jury of the district where the offense was committed, and fined not less than fifty nor more than one hundred dollars, and shall also pay all damages done said buildings; and in case of his, her or their inability to pay said fine and damages, he, she or they shall receive not less than fifty nor more than one hundred lashes on the bare back, and this act shall take effect and be in force from and after its passage.

APPROVED, November 10, 1887.

THOMPSON McKINNEY, P. C. C. N.

BILL NO. XXIV.

An Act amendatory of the Act of Nov. 9, 1875, in reference to intermarriage:

Be it enacted by the General Council of the Choctaw Nation assembled, That the Act of Nov. 9, 1875, in regard to the intermarriage of White men with the Choctaw women is hereby so amended, that County Clerks only shall issue license for such marriage, and instead of the White man paying Twenty-Five Dollars, they shall hereafter pay One Hundred Dollars and the County Clerks receiving said One Hundred Dollars and issuing the license, shall be allowed to retain Two and 50-100 Dollars of the same as their fees, and the remainder they shall turn into the County Treasuries of their respective Counties. In all other respects the laws of Nov. 9, 1875, shall be complied with and this Act shall take effect and be in force from and after its passage.

APPROVED Nov. 10, 1887.

THOMPSON McKINNEY, P. C. C. N.

BILL NO. XXV.

An act declaiming the late compilation, translation and publication of the Choctaw laws to be laws of the Choctaw Nation, in force at the time of their publication.

WHEREAS, By an act of the General Council, approved November 3, 1885, provision was made for the publication of the laws of the Choctaw Nation, and a committee was constituted and consisted of the Principal Chief, National Secretary and National Attorney, to award contracts for the compilation, translation and publication, and required bonds for their faithful performance of the work to be done under those contracts.

AND WHEREAS, Said committee did award said contracts, receive the work done under them, issue certificates to the various parties for their pay, and the work has all been paid for ;

Therefore the following shall be the enacting clause of said publication:

Be it enacted by the General Council of the Choctaw Nation assembled, that the said publication is hereby declared to contain the laws of the Choctaw Nation at the time of said publication, and they shall be obeyed and respected accordingly ; and this act shall take effect and be in force from and after its passage..

APPROVED, October 30, 1888.

B. F. SMALLWOOD,
P. C. C. N.

BILL XXVI.

An act declaiming the time when officers shall qualify.

Be it enacted by the General Council of the Choctaw Nation assembled, That all district and county officers who receive their certificates of election from the Supreme Judges, shall take the oath of office and enter upon the discharge of their duties on the 1st day of October next succeeding the election at which they are chosen, and shall hold office for two years unless removed for cause.

Be it further enacted, That all officers who are elected by the joint ballot of the Senate and House of Representatives, together with all officers appointed by the Chief by and with the advice and consent of the Senate, shall qualify and enter upon the discharge of their duties on the 1st day of November succeeding their election or appointment.

Be it further enacted, That all officers now holding shall continue in office, if they are elected by the people, until October 1, 1890, and those elected by the Council or appointed by the Chief until November 1, 1890.

Be it further enacted. That this act shall not apply to Senators or Representatives, Principal Chief or any member of his cabinet, Circuit and Supreme Judges, and that this act shall be in force from and after its passage.

APPROVED, November 6, 1888.

B. F. SMALLWOOD,
P. C. C. N.

BILL XXVII.

An act in reference to pay of witnesses.

Be it enacted by the General Council of the Choctaw Nation assembled, That in addition to the fees and mileage already allowed witnesses by the law of October 26, 1883, to be paid in county script, they shall be allowed one dollar per day while attending circuit court on behalf of the Nation, until discharged, in all criminal cases, and in civil cases where the Nation is a party in interest, to be paid out of the national treasury, on the certificates of the Judges of the Courts and attested by the Clerks, with the seals of the courts attached; provided, that in no case the costs in a civil suit between individuals are to be paid out of the national treasury, and provided further, that no officer, prisoner or other person, whose business takes him or her to court without a summons, or who happens to be present, not having been summoned, shall be allowed the above per diem for simply testifying in a case.

The act of November 7, 1887, is hereby repealed, and this act shall take effect and be in force from and after its passage.

APPROVED, November 6, 1888.

B. F. SMALLWOOD, P. C. C. N.

BILL XXVIII.

An act providing for three more students to be sent to school in the States.

Be it enacted by the General Council of the Choctaw Nation

assembled, That paragraph six of the law in reference to students to be sent to the states to school, on page 61 of the late compilation and revision of the Choctaw laws is hereby stricken out, and the following substituted in its stead: The Superintendent of Public schools is hereby authorized and instructed to select fifteen boys and twelve girls to be sent to school in the States, the same to be divided according to sex, equally among the several districts of the Choctaw Nation, and this act shall take effect from and after its passage.

APPROVED, November 1, 1888.

B. F. SMALLWOOD,
P. C. C. N.

BILL XXIX.

An act in reference to permits.

Be it enacted by the General Council of the Choctaw Nation assembled, That no permit shall be issued to any one keeping saloons, billiard halls or tables. Pool rooms or tables, or any kind of gambling in the Choctaw Nation is hereby prohibited, and that no non-citizen shall have the right to take out a permit for another non-citizen, and all laws or parts of laws in conflict with this act are hereby repealed, and this act shall take effect and be in force from and after its passage.

APPROVED, November 6, 1888.

B. F. SMALLWOOD,
P. C. C. N.

BILL XXX.

An act to prevent hunting, gathering or running cattle on Sunday.

Be it enacted by the General Council of the Choctaw Nation assembled, That the law in reference to hunting on Sunday, found on page 170, section 36, of the new compilation and revision of Choctaw laws, is hereby amended by adding the following language to line 2: Or to hunt, gather or run cattle on Sunday, provided, however, this act shall not be so construed as to prevent watching and caring for stock already under herd when overtaken by a Sunday, and this act shall take effect and be in force from and after its passage.

APPROVED, November 2, 1888.

B. F. SMALLWOOD,
P. C. C. N.

BILL XXXI.

An act to amend the law of November 1, 1882, in reference to coal weighers.

Be it enacted by the General Council of the Choctaw Nation assembled, That in line 3, first paragraph of the law in reference to coal weighers, on page 89, of the late compilation and revision of the Choctaw laws, the word "point" shall be stricken out and the words "mine shaft or opening" substituted instead; and in line 4 (four), of same paragraph, and same page, after the word "there" shall be inserted the following: And they shall be compelled to be at their places of weighing from 7 o'clock a. m. until 5 o'clock p. m., or during the time that the company weighmen and check weighmen are on duty, and it shall be the duty of the national agent to report all failures herein to the Principal Chief, and this act shall take effect and be in force from and after its passage.

APPROVED, October 26, 1888.

B. F. SMALLWOOD,
P. C. C. N.

BILL XXXII.

An Act to prohibit the leasing or renting pastures.

SECTION 1. Be it enacted by the General Council of the Choctaw Nation assembled, That it shall not be lawful for any person to rent or to lease a pasture to any other person for the purpose of grazing or pasturing cattle or stock of any kind.

SEC. 2. Any person violating this Act, shall on conviction be fined in any sum not less than two hundred and fifty dollars ($250), nor more than five hundred dollars, ($500), to be paid into the National Treasury for general purposes and the pasture so rented or leased be sold to satisfy said fine and cost if the person be unable otherwise to satisfy the same.

SEC. 3. That this Act shall take effect and be in force from and after its passage.

APPROVED, October, 26, 1888.

B. F. SMALLWOOD,
P. C. C. N.

BILL XXXIII.

An Act to provide Interpreters for both houses of the General Council.

Be it enacted by the General Council of the Choctaw Nation assembled, That the Senate and house of Representatives shall each be entitled to an interpreter to be elected by their respective houses as the door keeper and other officers, who shall take an oath of office which shall be administered by the presiding officer of the house, to which he is elected and who shall receive the same per diem as the members of their respective houses. It shall be the duty of said interpreters to be on hand at all sessions or meetings of their respective houses and do all interpreting required by any member thereof, and this Act shall take effect and be in force from and after its passage.

APPROVED, October 26, 1888.

B. F. SMALLWOOD,
P. C. C. N.

BILL XXXIV.

An Act amendatory of an Act to provide for the security of the National Treasury.

Be it enacted by the General Council of the Choctaw Nation assembled that Section 2 of an Act to provide for the Security of the National Treasury approved November, 9, 1887, is hereby amended so that the two light-horsemen to be subject to the order of the Treasuer, shall be in addition to the nine light-horsemen formerly provided for, and this Act shall take effect and be in force from and after its passage.

APPROVED, October 16, 1888.

B. F. SMALLWOOD,
P. C. C. N.

BILL XXXV.

An Act amendatory of an Act of November 6, 1880, in reference to the time coal contracts shall run.

Be it enacted by the General Council of the Choctaw Nation assembled, That on page 85 of the late compilation of the Choctaw Laws in the eighth line and immediatly after the words, "Mining Coal" there shall be inserted the words: "and quarrying stone" so that when amended the law shall read. All Contracts made hereunder shall expire on the 31st day of December, of each year, except for mining coal and quarrying stone which shall cover a period of six years, and all royalty accrueing under the same shall be due and payable monthly, and this Act so amended shall take effect and be in force from and after its passage.

APPROVED, October 15, 1888.

B. F. SMALLWOOD,
P. C. C. N.

BILL XXXVI.

An Act establishing Election Precinct in Atoka County C. N.

Be it enacted by the General Council of the Choctaw Nation assembled, That an Election Precinct is hereby established in Atoka County at a point about forty miles from the town of Atoka a little west of North and about one mile South of Auston Weaver's, which shall be called and known as Red Oak Hill Precinct, and this Act shall take effect and be in force from and after its passage.

APPROVED, October 22, 1888.

B. F. SMALLWOOD,
P. C. C. N.

BILL XXXVII.

An Act establishing an election Precinct in Atoka County C. N.

Be it enacted by the General Council of the Choctaw Nation assembled, That an election Precinct is hereby established in Atoka County, Choctaw Nation, about twenty seven miles north east of Atoka at a school house, about five miles west of Kiowa known as Little Boggy School house about one hundred yards from George Lowry's residence, and said Precinct shall be called and known as Little Boggy Precinct, and this Act shall take effect and be in force from and after its passage.

APPROVED, October 26, 1888.

B. F. SMALLWOOD,
P. C. C. N.

BILL XXXVIII.

An Act for the benefit of crippled, blind and idiotic.

Be it enacted by the General Council of the Choctaw Nation assembled, That each person, citizens of the Choctaw Nation so crippled as to be unable to keep themselves and having no property, blind or idiotic shall be entitled to fifty dollars payable out of the National Treasury, on the certificate (under the direction and discretion) of their respective County Judges, who are hereby authorized and required to see that the money is used for the beneficiaries under this Act, and all Laws or parts of Laws heretofore passed conflicting with this Act are hereby repealed, and this Act take effect and be in force from and after its passage.

APPROVED, November 7, 1888.

B. F. SMALLWOOD,
P. C. C. N.

XXXIX

An Act suspending the militia Law.

Be it enacted by the General Council of the Choctaw Nation assembled, That the law passed and approved November 1,

1883, creating the militia for the Choctaw Nation be and the same is hereby suspended, and that this Act take effect and be in force from and after its passage.

APPROVED, November 28, 1888.

B. F. SMALLWOOD,
P. C. C. N.

BILL XL.

An act requiring the manner of application for citizenship.

Be it enacted by the General Council of the Choctaw Nation assembled, That hereafter all claimants for citizenship in the Choctaw Nation shall pay into the national treasury the sum of one hundred dollars for each person asked to be adopted, and that no petition shall be entertained by the committee for citizenship unless accompanied by the National Treasurer's receipt as above required, and that this act shall take effect and be in force from and after its passage.

APPROVED, November 6, 1888.

B. F. SMALLWOOD,
P. C. C. N.

BILL XLI.

An act requiring the M., K. & T. Ry. Co. to reduce the rates of mileage on their line of railroad through the Indian Territory.

WHEREAS, The Gulf, Colorado & Santa Fe Railroad and St. Louis & San Francisco line of railroad have been required by the Congress of the United States to charge only three cents per mile as rates of mileage through the Indian Territory, and

WHEREAS, The M., K. & T. Ry. Company has been (since it constructed said line of railroad through the Indian Territory), charging the rates of five cents per mile, and should be required by an act of the General Council, to be approved by the Interior Department, to reduce the rates from five cents per mile to that of three cents per mile, as required of other lines of railroads through the Choctaw Nation, therefore

SEC. 1. Be it enacted by the General Council of the Choctaw Nation assembled, That the M., K. & T. R. R. Co. be and it is hereby required to reduce the rates of fare from five cents per mile, as charged heretofore, to three cents per mile, as are required of other companies operating lines of railway through the Choctaw Nation.

SEC. 2. Be it further enacted, That a certified copy of this act be forwarded by the National Secretary to the Hon. Secretary of the Interior for his approval.

SEC. 3. Be it further enacted, That this act shall take effect and be in force from and after its passage.

APPROVED, October 23, 1889.

BILL XLII.

An act changing an election precinct in Kiamichi County, Choctaw Nation.

SEC. 1. Be it enacted by the General Council of the Choctaw Nation assembled, That an election precinct in Kiamichi County, heretofore known as Clear Spring election precinct, is hereby changed and removed to Good Land station in said county, to be called and known hereafter as Good Land precinct.

SEC. 2. Be it further enacted, That the first election held at said Good Land precinct shall be on the first Wednesday in August, 1890, and thereafter, and that this act shall take effect and be in force from and after its passage.

APPROVED, October 28, 1889.

BILL XLIII.

An act changing Clear Spring court ground in Kiamichi County, Choctaw Nation.

SEC. 1. Be it enacted by the General Council of the Choctaw Nation assembled, That Clear Spring court ground in Kiamichi County be and is hereby changed and removed to Good Land station, on the St. Louis & San Francisco Railway, in said county, to be hereafter called and known as Good Land court ground.

SEC. 2. Be it further enacted, That in holding the first court at the said Good Land court ground it shall begin on the first Monday in January, 1890, and the first Monday in each month thereafter the year round.

SEC. 3. Be it further enacted, That the County Judge of said county is hereby authorized and required to appoint two or more competent persons to sell the former court house at Clear Springs, who shall first give public notice thirty days previous to the sale, in at least three public places in the county, and that the proceeds of such sale shall be set apart for the building of a new court house at Good Land, above mentioned.

SEC. 4. Be it further enacted, That this act shall take effect and be in force from and after its passage.

APPROVED, October 28, 1889.

BILL XLIV.

An act to appeal the act of citizenship, approved October 1, 1882.

TO THE GENERAL COUNCIL:—Your committee to whom was referred the recommendation of the Principal Chief, to repeal the act approved October 21, 1882, relative to appeal from the decision of the General Council of the Choctaw Nation, on the application of any person claiming the right of citizenship, have had the same under due and careful consideration, and recommend the passage of the following act, to-wit:

Be it enacted by the General Council of the Choctaw Nation assembled, That the decision of the General Council, on the application for citizenship by any person claiming the right of citizenship, shall be final, and that the act approved October 21, 1882, is hereby repealed in whole, and this act shall take effect and be in force from and after its passage.

APPROVED, October 30, 1889.

BILL XLV.

An Act suspending an Act making distribution of the Net Proceed Money.

SECTION 1. Be it enacted by the General Council of the Choctaw Nation assembled, That the law passed and approved

November 6, 1888, creating a commission for the distribution of the Net Proceeds Money; also, an Act amendatory to an Act approved January 18, 1889, be and the same is hereby suspended.

SEC. 2. Be it further enacted, That the said Net Proceeds Commission is by this Act required to file with the National Secretary all the books, records, dockets and all other papers belonging to said Commission's office for the inspection of the General Council, and that this Act take effect and be in force from and after its passage.

APPROVED, October 30, 1889.

BILL XLVI.

Joint Resolution of the Choctaw General Council.

WHEREAS, It has been reported to this body from reliable sources, and has been publicly announced in the newspapers upon the authority of the officers of the St. Louis & San Francisco Railway, that the said company has prepared a bill to be presented to the next session of the congress of the United States, asking that rights of way through the Indian Territory be granted by the said congress to a corporation known as the California & St. Louis Railway, said corporation being owned and controlled by the said St. Louis & San Francisco company system.

AND WHEREAS, The rights of way asked for aggregate more than two thousand miles and cover every section of the Indian Territory available for railway purposes, also paralleling rights of way already granted by congress and lines of railway now building or in progress of construction, and practically constitute a monopoly of the railway business in the said Indian Territory, and grants the same to California & St. Louis & San Francisco Railway otherwise known as the St. Louis & San Francisco Railway, to the exclusion of all competitors and to the consequent injury of citizens of the said Indian Territory;

AND WHEREAS, By the terms of the Treaty made by the United States with the five Indian tribes in the year 1866, which provided that one right of way should be granted for a railway north and south through the said Indian Territory, and one right of way east and west through the said Indian Territory;

AND WHEREAS, The north and south right of way has been taken by the Missouri, Kansas & Texas Railway, a line of railway constructed thereon, and a line of railway east and west has been taken by the Choctaw Coal and Railway company, which said company is constructing a line of railway thereon;

AND WHEREAS, In addition to these railways provided for in the Treaty of 1866 the congress of the United States has granted to other railways at different times, right of way through the said Indian Territory, some of which have actually been built upon and others are now building;

AND WHEREAS, The public policy demands that the business of this Territory shall be given to no one corporation to the exclusion of all others and the Territory obligations of the United States having been violated by the giving of other rights of railway than those provided for in the Treaty of 1866; now, therefore,

Be it resolved by the General Council of the Choctaw Nation in joint session assembled, That we hereby solemnly protest against the granting of the right of way asked for by the said California & St. Louis Railway, otherwise known as the St. Louis & San Francisco Railway Company as being a subversion of all the rights of Indian citizens and as having a tendency to destroy that competition which has been inaugurated by the granting of the rights of way to others than those provided for in the Treaty.

And we desire to respectfully represent to the congress of the United States that if the St. Louis & San Francisco Railway, otherwise known as the California & St. Louis Railway be granted the rights asked for it will practically end railway building outside of that company in the Territory, and leave the citizens of the five nations at the mercy of one corporation in all future railway developments.

And we further declare that in our opinion, based upon the record of the St. Louis & San Francisco Railway in this Territory in the past, that the said railways for which the rights of way are to be asked in the proposed bill, and that the corporation is asking for the same for the purpose of intimidating other corporations seeking to do business in the Territory and to retard the development of competitive systems.

And we further respectfully represent to the congress of the United States that the said St. Louis & San Francisco Railway has held over twenty years' right of way through this Territory upon which it has never built and is not now engaged in building.

Be it further resolved, That a certified copy of this joint resolution be forwarded by the National Secretary of the Choctaw Nation to the President of the United States, to the Honorable Secretary of the Interior, to the President of the Senate and Speaker of the House of Representatives of the United States of America.

Be it further resolved, That this resolution shall take effect and be in force from and after its passage.

APPROVED, Nov. 5, 1889.

BILL XLVII.

An Act authorizing the appointment of three commissioners to treat with U. S. Commissioners in reference to the Leased District, and for other purposes.

WHEREAS, By Act of Congress May 28, 1830, the President of the United States was authorized to set apart a certain country now the Indian Territory and solemnly assure the tribes to whom it was assigned that their heirs, or successors, might forever possess and occupy it; and whereas, pursuant to this Act of Congress the President of the United States the following September did make a treaty with the Choctaw Nation assigning to it a tract including their present country, which was subsequently patented to them; and whereas, by the 9th article of the Treaty of 1855, the Choctaws and Chickasaws leased to the United States all that portion of their common territory west of the 98th degree of longitude for the Wichita and such other tribes or bands of Indians as the government might desire to locate thereon, reserving however the right to the Choctaws and Chickasaws to settle thereon; and whereas, on the 9th of September, 1865, Hon. D. N, Cooley, Commissioner of Indian Affairs, Hon. Elijah Sells, Superintendent Southern Superintendency, Thomas Wister, of the Society of Friends, Brigadier General W. S. Harney, United States Army, and Colonel Ely S. Parker, of General Grant's staff, appointed by the President of the United States as a board of commissioners, did, as the declared and acknowledged representatives of the President of the United States, duly empowered, declare to the commissioners of the Choctaw Nation that the new treaty must contain among other things the following stipulations, to-wit:

5th. That a portion of the lands hitherto owned and occupied by the Choctaws and Chickasaws must be set apart for the friendly tribes then in Kansas and elsewhere, and on the further stipulation:

7th. That no white person except officers, agents and employees of the Government, or of any internal improvement authorized by the government would be permitted to reside in the Territory unless formerly incorporated with some tribe according to the usages of the bands; and whereas, on the representations of the said United States Commissioners that the lands west of the 98th degree of west longitude on which the Choctaws and Chickasaws had still the right to settle, would all be needed for the use of friendly Indians and the colonization of the Negro freedmen in the Chickasaw and Choctaw Nations, unless otherwise adopted by the Choctaws and Chickasaws, the Choctaw and Chickasaw Nation did by the 3rd article of the treaty of 1866, cede the lands west of the 98th degree of west longitude to the United States, in trust, for the purposes aforesaid, and under the conditions of the existing laws and treaties of the United States herein before mentioned.

AND WHEREAS, By act of Congress of March 1, 1889, the United States departed from the long established policy of holding the lands of the Indian Territory for Indian settlement, by purchase of the lands of the Creeks and Seminoles, which had been sold to the United States for the same purposes as in the case of the Choctaw cession of the lands west of the 98th degree of west longitude;

AND WHEREAS, The United States by act of Congress of

March 2, 1889, in pursuance of this new line of policy, authorized the President of the United States to appoint three commissioners to negotiate with all Indians owning or claiming lands lying west of the 96th degree of west longitude in the Indian Territory for cessions to the United States of all of their title, claim or interest of every kind or character in and to said lands;

AND WHEREAS, The Choctaw people recognize the changes which have taken place in the policy of the United States, and the desire of the government to establish a Territorial government in the western part of the Indian Territory, and the need to use the lands west of the 98th degree of west longitude for a different purpose than the holding in trust for friendly Indians, as by the cessions of 1866;

AND WHEREAS, The Choctaws have been willing and anxious to conform to the wishes of the United States, consistently with the interests of their own people, now, therefore,

SECTION 1. Be it enacted by the General Council of the Choctaw Nation assembled, That the Principal Chief of the Choctaw Nation is hereby authorized and directed to appoint, by and with the advice of the Senate, three competent, sober men, who shall constitute a commission to represent the Choctaw Nation in reference to the rights of the Nation in the lands lying between the 98th and 100th degrees of west longitude, and between the Red and Canadian rivers, comprising an area of 7,713,230 acres.

SEC. 2. Said commissioners are hereby authorized and directed to conduct negotiations with the United States commissioners in accordance with the Act of Congress of March 2, 1889, or with other proper authorities of the United States for the cession to the United States of all the claims, interest, and title of the Choctaw Nation in and to the lands lying west of 98th degree of west longitude.

Said commissioners are hereby instructed to actively and strenuously oppose and resist any attempt to include these lands within the limits of the proposed Oklahoma Territory until the Choctaw Nation shall have their rights therein properly recognized and secured.

SEC. 3. Said commissioners are also hereby instructed to invite the co-operation of the Chickasaw Nation in the purpose of this Act, and to report at once to the Principal Chief any agreement arrived at with the authorities of the United States; provided, however, that no agreement of the said commission shall be binding until duly ratified by the General Council, and it shall be the duty of the Principal Chief to immediately convene the General Council on receiving notice that an agreement has been reached by the commission herein provided for.

SEC. 4. Said commissioners shall be allowed for their services, six dollars per day, and mileage of ten cents per mile while on this National business, payable on their own certificate, approved by the Principal Chief, and a sum sufficient to defray such expenses is hereby appropriated out of any money in the Treasury not otherwise appropriated.

Be it further enacted, That this Act shall take effect and be in force from and after its passage.

APPROVED, November 5, 1889.

BILL XLVIII.

An Act repealing a portion of the preamble of "An Act authorizing the appointment of three commissioners to treat with U. S. Commissioners in reference to the Leased District," and for other purposes, approved Nov. 5, 1889.

Be it enacted by the General Council of the Choctaw Nation assembled, That all that portion of the preamble of the Act authorizing the appointment of the commissioners to treat with U. S. Commissioners in reference to the Leased District, and for other purposes, approved Nov. 5, 1889, which reads, "And whereas, the Choctaws, by treaty of 1837, sold to the Chickasaws a one-fourth interest in all of their lands" be and the same is hereby repealed, and this act shall take effect and be in force from and after its passage.

APPROVED. November 9, 1889.

BILL XLIX.

An Act entitled an Act repealing an Act to prohibit introducing steer cattle in the Choctaw Nation.

Be it enacted by the General Council of the Choctaw Nation assembled, That an Act heretofore passed and become a law by its own limitation on the 30th of October, 1888, to prohibit introducing steer cattle in the Choctaw Nation, except in the months of November and December, is hereby repealed.

And that this Act shall take effect and be in force from and after its passage.

APPROVED November 13, 1889.

BILL L.

An Act changing the county court ground of Wade County.

Be it enacted by the General Council of the Choctaw Nation assembled, That the county court ground of Wade County is hereby removed from what is known as Kochot owa Kah Court grounds to Tali Hina, and it shall be called and known as Tali Hina Court ground.

The County Court of Wade county shall hold its first session at Tali Hina Court ground on the first Monday in January, 1890, and this act shall take effect and be in force from and after the 31st day of December, 1889.

APPROVED, November 13, 1889.

BILL LI.

An Act instructing the Principal Chief to call upon the Interior Department for certain information.

Be it enacted by the General Council of the Choctaw Nation assembled, That the Principal Chief is hereby instructed to call upon the Interior Department for a detailed statement of the expenditure and disbursement of the Choctaw freedmen fund placed in the hands of Robert L. Owen, U. S. Indian Agent, for payment to such Choctaw freedmen as appeared and elected to leave the Nation in accordance with the third article of the Treaty of 1866, and besides the numbers and names of those paid, ascertain how many remain unpaid, and what has been done with the money, if any, returned by the U. S. Indian

Agent, and this act shall take effect and be in force from and after its passage.

APPROVED, November 13, 1889.

BILL LII.

An Act to provide for Protection of the Rights of the Choctaw Nation and her Citizens against Increased Encroachments by U. S. Courts.

WHEREAS, In pursuance of a custom long established among the Choctaws and of the 38th article of the Treaty of 1866, white persons who intermarry with Choctaw citizens became entitled to all the rights and privileges of citizenship in the Choctaw Nation, to vote and hold office, to sue and be sued in the Choctaw courts, to be tried for offenses and punished in all respects as though they were native born Choctaws; and whereas, Stephen Belvin, a Choctaw citizen by blood, being charged with the killing of one A. E. Powell, a white man, and citizen of the Choctaw Nation by intermarriage, and had been arrested by the Choctaw authorities and held for his appearance at the regular February term of the circuit court of the Third district of the Choctaw Nation for trial; and whereas, the said Stephen Belvin has been arrested for the same offense and held for trial by the district court of the U. S., holding session at Paris, in disregard of the said 38th article of the Treaty of 1866, and disregard of the rights of the said Belvin and of the Choctaws; and

WHEREAS, A case of a precisely similar nature has been taken into the U. S. courts at Paris, Texas, against Captain Joe Everidge, Turner Everidge and Martin Everidge, charged with the killing of one Luther, a white man, but a citizen by intermarriage, and the defendants are held there under bond; and whereas, in pursuance of the laws of the Choctaw Nation of October 30, 1877, and October 28, 1887, Joe Nale, Sheriff of Tobucksy County, in pursuance of his duties under said laws, and in pursuance of instructions of the U. S. Indian Agent, sold some houses in the town of Krebs, C. N., the property of non-citizens—intruders—and disposed of them, they being illegally there and pursuing an illegitimate business in them, and whereas, in consequence suit has been brought in the U. S. court at Muskogee against the said Joe Nale for the value of the houses sold, and damages, by the non-citizens; and

WHEREAS, Suit has been brought in the court at Muskogee against Adolphus Riddle, administrator of the estate of Mick Nichols, deceased, of Jacks Fork County, and a citizen of the Choctaw Nation, by intermarriage, at the instance of one Huggins, a citizen of the State of Arkansas, and the property of said estate has been attached by the said court and the property taken from the custody of the said Adolphus Riddle and ordered to be sold at auction to the highest bidder for cash, to the great detriment of the interest of said estate and in utter disregard of the jurisdiction of the Choctaw courts; and whereas, Sam Harris, a registered freedman of the Choctaw Nation, became involved in a difficulty with and killed Sam Brown, also a registered freedman of the Choctaw Nation, both being residents of Towson County, and the case clearly coming within the jurisdiction of the courts of the Choctaw Nation. as in such cases decided by Judge Parker, of the Fort Smith court, in the case of Morris Green et al., from Gaines County; and whereas, the said Sam Harris is held for trial by the United States court at Paris, Texas; therefore,

Be it enacted by the General Council of the Choctaw Nation assembled. That the Principal Chief of the Choctaw Nation is hereby authorized to employ the firm of Guthridge, Fleming & Co., of Paris, Texas, to appear in said courts and represent the interest of the Choctaw Nation by pleading to jurisdiction of said courts in all such cases, or to take such course as may be necessary in the defense of the Treaty and other rights of the Choctaw Nation and her citizens, and for their services they shall receive the sum of fifteen hundred dollars, to be paid on the certificate of the Principal Chief whenever it shall have been satisfactorily proven to him to be justly due. The said amount of money to be paid out of any money in the treasury not otherwise appropriated, and this act shall take effect and be in force from and after its passage.

APPROVED, November 14, 1889.

BILL LIII.

An Act to Increase the Pay of County Officers.

Be it enacted by the General Council of the Choctaw Nation assembled, That the pay of county officers of the Choctaw Nation is increased as follows.

County Judges, - - - - - -	$100 00
County Clerks, - - - - - - -	50 00
Sheriffs and their Deputies, each - - -	50 00

These amounts to be in addition to what is already allowed them, and this act shall take effect and be in force from and after its passage.

APPROVED, November 14, 1889.

B'LL LIV.

An Act changing an election precinct in Kiamitia County.

Be it enacted by the General Council of the Choctaw Nation assembled, That the election precinct know as Lockston precinct in Kiamitia County, is hereby discontinued, and instead, there is hereby established one-half mile South of the said Lockston precinct, at what is known as Saw Mill Church, a precinct which shall be called and known as Saw Mill Church, and this Act shall take effect and be in force from and after its passage.

APPROVED, November 20, 1889.

B. F. SMALLWOOD, P. C. C. N.

BILL LV.

An Act amending an Act in reference to the Scholars attending boarding schools.

SECTION 1. Be it enacted by the General Council of the Choctaw Nation assembled, That the Act of November 1842, as found in paragraph 4, section 5, chapter 1, at the top of page 67 of the late compilation of Choctaw laws, and which reads as follows:

"No family shall be allowed to have more than one scholar

in the boarding schools of the Choctaw Nation," shall be and is hereby amended to read as follows:

No family shall be allowed to have more than one scholar at schools in the States or in the boarding schools of the Choctaw Nation at the expense of the Choctaw Nation.

SEC. 2: In all cases wherein any family may have more than one scholar at school in the states, or in a boarding school of the Nation, the Superintendent of Public Schools shall revoke the certificate of all but one, and proceed at once to fill any vacancies created thereby. This Act shall take effect from and after the first day of August 1890, and be in force thereafter.

APPROVED, December 20, 1889.

B. F. SMALLOOD, P. C., C. N.

BILL LVI.

An Act to provide for further development of the mineral resources of the Choctaw Nation.

WHEREAS, There is a growing necessity for increase of the funds of the Choctaw Nation to meet the demands for education and all elevating agencies ; and whereas those minerals which are undiscovered in the bowels of the earth can be of no posible benefit to the present or future generations unless they find development and are operated , Therefore,

Be it enacted by the General Council of the Choctaw Naion assembled, That any citizen of the Choctaw Nation who shall discover Lead, Iron or other metal, or mineral than coal, shall be allowed the exclusive privilege of working the same within a radius of one mile from the point of discovery, provided that he shall duly record the same in the office of the county clerk of the county wherein the same metal or mineral may be located.

Provided, further, that he shall pay a royalty on the same to the Choctaw and Chickasaw Nations of 6 per cent., three-fourths to the Choctaw and one-fourth to the Chickasaw Nation of said 6 per cent of the value of the metal or mineral when it is prepared for the general market; and provided, further, that he shall be required to enter into contract with the National Agent of the Choctaw Nation on the same terms, conditions and penalties as simular contracts are made for the mining of coal.

APPROVED, December 23, 1889.

B. F. SMALLWOOD, P. C. C. N.

BILL LVII.

An Act relating to citizens of the Choctaw Nation taking the oath of allegiance to the United States.

Be it enacted by the General Council of the Choctaw Nation assembled, That any member of the Choctaw tribe of Indians, either by blood, adoption, or by marriage into said tribe and subject to the government of the Choctaw Nation, who has taken or may hereafter take the oath of allegiance to the government of the United States, shall be disqualified to hold any office of trust or profit in the Choctaw Nation, and to vote at any election in said Nation, and to be impanneled as a juror in any court under the government of said Choctaw Nation.

This Act shall take effect from and after its passage.

APPROVED, October 25, 1890.

W. N. JONES,
P. C. C. N.

BILL LVIII.

Amendment to Section 2 of the Act of November 1, 1882, in regard to shipping hay.

Be it enacted by the General Council of the Choctaw Nation assembled, That from and after the passage of this Act a royalty is hereafter levied on all prairie or wild grass cut for sale or barter, whether upon a public domain or within citizens' enclosures.

The sheriff of each county shall collect said royalty and pay the same, less 10 per cent for his services, to the County Treasurer for county purposes of the county in which such grass shall have been cut.

Nothing herein contained as to impose a royalty on grass

cut by any citizen for his own use, and this act take effect from and after its passage.

APPROVED, October 30, 1890.

W. N. JONES,
P. C. C. N.

BILL LIX.

An Act to abolish Good Spring and Cole Spring Precincts in Blue County and to establish Jones' Precinct instead.

Be it enacted by the General Council of the Choctaw Nation assembled, That Good Spring precinct and Cole Spring precinct, located in Blue county, be and the same are hereby abolished.

Be it further enacted, That an election precinct is hereby established at Cornelius Jones' house, in Blue county, and shall be called and known as Jones' precinct, and voters may vote at said precinct. And this act shall take effect and be in force from and after its passage.

APPROVED, October 30, 1890.

W. N. JONES,
P. C. C. N.

BILL LX.

An Act changing boundary lines of certain counties.

Be it enacted by the General Council of the Choctaw Nation assembled, That the boundary line of Wade county shall be as follows, to-wit: Beginning on the top of the dividing ridge where the dividing line of Mosholittubbee District strikes the boundary line of the state of Arkansas, running thence along the top of the dividing ridge westward to where the road leading from Horse prairie to Fort Smith crosses the same; thence along said road to Jack's Fork, to its junction with Kiamitia; thence down Kiamitia to the narrows, one mile above Hoteka's place; thence on a straight line to a spring on the Kiamitia mountain, known as Okchaga's place; thence following a line on the top of the main Kiamitia mountain, eastwardly, to the

Arkansas line; thence along said line northwardly to the beginning.

SEC. 2. Be it further enacted, That the boundary lines of Cedar county are hereby changed, so that it will follow up Ward's creek to its junction with Little River to the source of said Ward's creek; thence in a northwardly direction on a straight line to the top of the main Kiamitia mountain to a junction with Wade county under the old boundary east of Ward's creek, and the line from its source to the top of Kiamitia mountain is hereby declared a part of Nashoba county, and all that portion on the west of said Ward's creek and the line is hereby declared a part of Cedar county.

SEC. 3. Be it enacted, That all former laws are hereby repealed, and this Act take effect and be in force from and after its passage.

APPROVED, October 31, 1890.

W. N. JONES,
P. C. C. N.

BILL LXI.

An Act relating to the School System of the Choctaw Nation.

Be it enacted by the General Council of the Choctaw Nation assembled:

BOARD OF EDUCATION.

CHAPTER I.

SECTION 1. There is hereby created a Board of Education of the Choctaw Nation, to be composed of the Principal Chief, who shall be ex-officio president of said Board, one Superintendent of Schools, and three (3) District Trustees, one from each District. The Superintendent of Schools and the District Trustees shall be elected by both houses of the General Council in joint session; shall hold office for the term of two years, and until their successors are qualified, and shall receive for compensation an annual salary as follows: The Superintendent, six hundred dollars ($600); each District Trustee, four hundred dollars ($400), to be paid quarterly out of the general funds of the Nation.

SEC. 2. Said Superintendent and District Trustees shall each, before entering upon the duties of their respective offices, give bond to the Choctaw Nation with at least two good sureties, in the sum of five thousand dollars ($5,000), to be approved by the Principal Chief, conditioned upon the faithful performance of all duties imposed on them by law. They shall each take the usual oath of officers of the Choctaw Nation.

SEC. 3. The powers and duties of the Board of Education shall be as follows, to wit:

1. To exercise a general supervisory control over the school system of the Choctaw Nation.

2. To make all necessary rules and regulations, not inconsistent with this act, for its own government and the government of the various Academies, Seminaries and neighborhood schools.

3. To examine and appoint all teachers as hereinafter provided.

4. To contract with superintendents of public schools ; but no such contract shall be valid unless approved by the Principal Chief and signed by at least three other members of the Board.

5. To revoke the certificate of any teacher for immoral, intemperate or improper conduct.

6. To prescribe the text books to be used in all schools.

7. To suspend any Academy or Seminary in case of general sickness or epidemic.

8. To discontinue any neighborhood school, should the same in their judgment be expedient.

9. To designate permanent locations for any or all the neighborhood schools, if in their judgment such action would promote the cause of education. Powers in paragraphs 8 and 9 may be delegated to respective District Trustees.

10. To prescribe the course of study in the various public schools, and it is made the duty of the Board to foster, as far as possible, in the Academies, manual training in the mechanical arts and theoretical and practical agriculture.

11. To select scholars to be sent to the states to school at

the public expense ; such scholars must be selected from those in attendance upon public schools ; they shall be selected from the various districts as nearly as may be in proportion to the school population of each, and the number of each sex shall be kept equal. They shall be examined by some competent physician selected by the Superintendent of Schools, and if physically disqualified, shall be rejected and others sent in the stead of such as may be rejected.

The Board of Education shall have a seal with the inscription, "Board of Education, Choctaw Nation." It shall keep a record of its proceedings, and its official acts shall be authenticated by its seal.

SEC. 4. It shall be the duty of the Board of Education to select one Superintendent and at least two teachers for each public school now, or hereafter to be erected in the Choctaw Nation. Advertisements shall be inserted in papers in at least three different states and in one paper in the Choctaw Nation, setting forth the duties, qualifications and emoluments of such Superintendents and teachers, other things being equal, preference shall be given to applicants professing Christianity. The teachers shall have at least ten years' experience in their profession, and must bring ample testimonials as to competency and morality. The male teachers must be graduates of some college of established reputation and capable of giving instruction in Greek, Latin, German and French. The females must be graduates of some higher institution of learning or some reputable normal school, and capable of instructing in two modern languages other than English. Upon the approval of this act, it shall be the duty of the Superintendent of Schools at once to notify the Superintendent of Public Schools in writing, that the Choctaw Nation elect to cancel all existing contracts at the expiration of the current scholastic year. He shall then begin to negotiate for new contracts. As to Academies, Seminaries or High Schools hereafter to be established, contracts will be made in accordance with the first paragraph of this Section and Section 5 of this Chapter.

Paragraph 2: as to public schools now in existence. The Board of Education may in its discretion, make contracts as heretofore subject to the general provisions of this act, with Boards of Home Missions, in which latter event, however, paragraph 1 of this Section and Section 5 of this Chapter shall not apply, nor will the Nation engage to pay the salaries of Superintendents or teachers in such schools. Such contracts shall also contain a clause authorizing either party to rescind the same upon six months' notice in writing to the other, and the absence of such stipulations shall render such contract void AB INITIO.

SEC. 5. The Superintendent of each of the public schools shall receive an annual salary of $1,200, to be paid in equal quarterly installments out of the general funds of the Choctaw Nation. The teachers in said public schools shall receive each an annual salary of not less than $750 and not more than $1,200, to be paid in like manner out of said general funds. The Superintendents shall hold their positions for six years, and the Board is authorized to make written contracts to that effect. Any Superintendent or teacher may, however, be discharged upon charges sustained by the Board; but such charges must be in writing; must be heard by the full Board. The party charged must have written notice of the time and place of investigation and given full opportunity to be heard in his or her own defense, and at least four members of the Board must concur in sustaining the charge and charges.

SEC. 6. All sums appropriated for the support and maintenance of the public schools shall be paid out to the respective Superintendents in equal installments on the first Mondays in September, November, February and May of each year. The Superintendent of schools shall make his requisition for such sums, under direction of the Board, upon the National Auditor, who shall thereupon issue his warrant for the same, said warrants shall be paid out of the respective appropriations by the National Treasurer any surplus remaining over at the expiration of the scholastic year, shall be returned by the Superintendent in whose schools such surplus shall exist, to the National Treasurer, and by him converted into the treasury. This section shall apply to all new contracts whatever with Superintendents of Public Schools.

SEC. 7. The Board of Education shall examine all applicants for the position of teacher in the neighborhood schools, but for this purpose the Principal Chief and each District Trustee may each select a proxy to represent him at such examination. Such proxies need not be citizens of the Choctaw Nation, but must be competent to conduct such examination. The applicants shall be examined in reading, writing, spelling and Grammar of the English language, in Geography and History, particularly of the United States; a fair knowledge of the Constitution of the United States and of the Choctaw Nation shall also be required. It is particularly enjoined upon the Board, in selecting teachers, that regard can be had to the disposition of applicants as far as the same can be determined by personal observation at the time of such examination. Upon the conclusion of the examinations in each district, each successful candidate shall be required to enter according to merit into one of the three grades to be known as "First," "Second" and "Third" Grades, the first being the highest. Each successful candidate shall receive a certificate from the Board, specifying his or her grade. Teachers shall be assigned by the Board, as near as may be, to the neighborhood school whence they are sent by the respective local trustees; but if any local trustee fails to send a candidate, or having sent one, such candidate fails to secure a certificate, then the Board shall send some other competent person to such neighborhood. The foregoing examination shall be conducted at least once in each district annually, and for their services in this behalf the members of the Board doing the actual labor shall receive each the sum of $5.00 per day and mileage at the rate of five (5) cents per mile for each mile actually traveled. Such examinations shall not be held more than five (5) days each year in each district. The times and places of such examinations shall be fixed previously by the Board, and at least three months' notice given thereof by advertisement in one newspaper published in the Nation, the expense to be paid out of the contingent fund of the Superintendent of Schools.

SEC. 8. The scholastic year of the public schools shall begin on the first Monday of September of each year, and shall close between the 10th and 30th of June. The Superintendent of Schools and three District Trustees shall attend the annual examination of each of said schools; and to this end the Board of Education shall, by regulation, fix the dates of the closing thereof in such wise as to enable said Superintendent and District Trustees to be personally present at all of said examinations.

SEC. 9. The Superintendent of Schools shall have an annual contingent fund of $450, and each District Trustee of $750, for the expenditure of which they must account to the full Board of Education at its annual meeting. All minor expenses not herein specifically provided for shall be paid out of the respective contingent funds.

SEC. 10. The full Board of Education shall meet at least once in every year in regular annual session. This meeting shall be at Tushka Humma, and shall begin during the first week of the regular annual session of the General Council; at such meeting the Board shall make up its annual report to said Council. Such report shall contain an itemized account of all expenditures on account of schools by said Board, or any of its members. It shall also contain a general review of the last scholastic year, the condition, progress and attendance at all schools, and such recommendations as to legislation as the Board may deem expedient or necessary. The Board shall transmit with its own report the reports of the various Superintendents of Public Schools.

SEC. 11. The President may call special sessions of the Board whenever he shall deem it necessary, to be held at such places as he may designate.

SUPERINTENDENT OF SCHOOLS.

CHAPTER II.

SECTION 1. The Superintendent of Schools shall be the executive officer of the Board of Education, and is charged with carrying into effect all orders, rules and regulations of said Board.

SEC. 2. He shall correspond with the principals of schools outside of the Nation, at which Choctaw pupils are attending, at the public expense, and with the scholars themselves, in order to acquaint himself with the progress and needs of such scholars.

DISTRICT TRUSTEE.

CHAPTER III.

SECTION 1. Each District Trustee shall have a seal of office, which shall bear on the outer edge the words, "District Trustee Choctaw Nation," and within the circle the Choctaw name of his district, followed by the word "District." As soon as qualified, each District Trustee shall write his signature in a book to be kept by the National Treasurer for that purpose. All certificates required by law to be made by a District Trustee shall be signed in person and his seal of office affixed to the same.

SEC. 2. The teachers of neighborhood schools shall be paid by the National Treasurer, upon monthly certificates of the District Trustee of the district in which such shall be located. Such certificate shall be made out upon the monthly report of each teacher when certified to by the local Trustee. Each District Trustee shall file all certified teachers' reports and present the same to the Board at its annual meeting, with his district report.

SEC. 3. The District Trustees shall also report to the Board, at its regular annual meeting, the names of all the scholars as reported to them by the local Trustees.

SEC. 4. Each District Trustee shall have power to suspend any neighborhood school in the district in time of general sickness or epidemic in the neighborhood.

SEC. 5. The District Trustees shall, each in his own district at once upon the receipt by him of any charges against any teacher in his district, to investigate the same, and if the charges are sustained to suspend the delinquent and appoint as a substitute any available person holding a certificate from the Board of Education.

LOCAL TRUSTEES.

CHAPTER IV.

SECTION 1. There shall be a Local Trustee in each neighborhood, who shall be the head of a family; shall be appointed by the District Trustee of his district; shall hold office for one scholastic year.

SEC. 2. It shall be the duty of the Local Trustee to select one competent person in his neighborhood who may be a non-citizen and send him or her to the annual teachers' examination in his district. He shall visit his school at least once a month, and at the end of each month he shall examine the teacher's report and account, and if the same be correct, he shall so certify. Such account and certificate shall be sent by the teacher to the District Trustee. He shall report to the District Trustee any improper conduct on the part of the teacher for investigation as provided in the act.

It shall be the duty of all Local Trustees to uphold teachers in enforcing proper discipline in the neighborhood school, and to enjoin upon pupils the necessity of showing due respect to the teacher.

SEC. 3. Local Trustees shall receive no compensation for their services.

SEC. 4. Local Trustees shall enroll all children in their respective neighborhoods between the ages of seven and eighteen, and report the same to the proper District Trustee at the end of each scholastic year.

NEIGHBORHOOD SCHOOLS.

CHAPTER V.

SECTION 1. Any neighborhood that can employ a teacher shall be entitled to a neighborhood school; provided, however, that such schools shall not be nearer to each other than three miles measured along the most direct traveled wagon road; and provided further, that this limitation as to distance shall not apply to acknowledged towns. The provisions of this section are subject to the powers conferred upon the Board of Education by Sec. 3, par. 8 and 9, Chap. I., of this act.

SEC. 2. Neighborhood schools shall be taught at least six (6) hours daily, Saturdays and Sundays excepted, during the term, and shall have regular hours of opening and closing. They shall open for the term on the first Monday of September and close on the last day of May of each year; but the District Trustee shall have power to grant short vacations and holidays at stated times during the term.

SEC. 3. The benefits of a free neighborhood school shall extend only to such Choctaw children as attend the schools within the Choctaw Nation established; and it is hereby made the duty of all Choctaw parents or guardians to send their children to school.

SEC. 4. The parents or guardians of all enrolled children who fail to send them to school shall be fined ten cents per day for each child enrolled who shall fail in attendance (not, however, to exceed $2.00 per child per month), except in cases of sickness, bad weather, or other casualty. The money shall be collected as provided in Sec. 5, Chap. VI., of this act (but in no case shall any sum be paid out of the County Treasury on this account), shall be paid into the contingent fund of the District Trustee of that district. In case of necessity or other good cause shown to the District Trustee, he may excuse any child from attendance upon the neighborhood schools for reasonable periods of time.

SEC. 5. Teachers in neighborhood schools shall be entitled to two dollars ($2.00) per month for each scholar in attendance, when such scholar has attended more than twenty days in the month. But where the attendance has been less than twenty (20) days, then such teacher shall receive 10 cents for each day of attendance; provided, however, that teachers of the First Grade shall not receive over forty-five dollars ($45) in any one month; those of the Second Grade not over thirty dollars ($30), and those of the Third Grade not over twenty dollars ($20).

SEC. 6. A scholastic month shall be taken and held to extend from a day of one calendar month to the corresponding day of the succeeding calendar month.

BOARDING SCHOOLS.

CHAPTER VI.

SECTION 1. The Superintendent of each boarding school in the Nation shall give a bond with at least two sureties, payable to the Principal Chief, and to be approved by him, in the sum of five thousand dollars ($5,000), conditioned upon the faithful performance of his duties as imposed by law, and observance of his contract with the Board of Education.

SEC. 2. The Superintendents shall take charge of their respective schools and conduct the same under the supervision of the Board of Education. They shall make full reports to the Board at the end of each scholastic year, which reports shall embody the names and ages of all scholars, with their percentage in each study, the attendance, and other matters connected with their progress and the internal discipline of the schools, together with an itemized statement of all moneys received and expended, accompanied with proper vouchers.

SEC. 3. The number of scholars at each of these schools shall be one hundred; at Spencer Academy they shall be boys, and at New Hope Seminary they shall be girls. One of each sex shall be chosen from the Choctaws residing in the Chickasaw country, ninety-nine of each sex shall be apportioned among the various counties in the Choctaw Nation by the Board of Education in proportion to the school population of said counties. The Board shall notify the County Judge of each county at least thirty days before the beginning of each scholastic year, how many pupils of each sex his county is entitled to; each County Judge shall then select his county's quota from the neighborhood schools, and give each person so selected, or to his or her parents or guardian, a certificate of such selection.

SEC. 4. Before admission each scholar shall be required to pass a creditable physical examination before some competent physician selected by the Superintendent of Schools, and also a mental examination, the standard of which shall be fixed by the Board. There shall be no limit as to age, though a regular course shall be held to be five years, but any pupil may be retained longer or sooner discharged by the Board upon recommendation by the Superintendent of either school.

SEC. 5. Upon selecting the scholars from his county each Judge shall forthwith notify the proper Superintendent of public schools of names and postoffice address of such scholars, and also the name and address of the Sheriff of his county. If any pupil to whom a certificate has been issued shall fail for ten (10) days after the opening of school, or, when the certificate was issued after the opening of school, for ten days after the proper Superintendent has been notified, to report to his or her school, it shall be the duty of the Superintendent of such school to notify the proper Sheriff of such failure. The Sheriff shall at once investigate the case, and if the pupil was not detained by high water, or sickness of self or family, then he shall take such pupil within five days to the proper school at the expense of parent or guardian. For this duty he shall be allowed $2.00 per day and five cents per mile for each mile actually traveled by each student and by himself by the usual traveled route. The Sheriff's account must be verified under oath, and if on demand, the parent or guardian refuse to pay the same, the Sheriff may take summary judgment in the circuit court of his district, upon a satisfactory showing to the Judge thereof, that the expenses were lawfully incurred, for the amount of his bill and costs, without further notice or demand against such parent or guardian. Upon such judgment execution shall issue forthwith. If such execution cannot be satisfied, then the Sheriff shall be paid out of the County Treasury where such execution debtor resides, upon the County Judge being satisfied of the correctness of the account. The county paying the account shall be subrogated to the Sheriff's rights under the execution. If there be more than one delinquent pupil in the same county, it shall be the duty of the Sheriff to take all such in one trip, and the circuit court shall not give judgment in any case where this provision appears not to have been complied with.

SEC. 6. No family shall have more than one scholar at any one time at the boarding schools of this Nation, nor in the states at the expense of the Nation.

ORPHAN SCHOOLS.

CHAPTER VII.

SECTION 1. There shall be fifty (50) orphan boys at Armstrong Academy and fifty girls at Wheelock Seminary. During vacation, such as have no relative or proper friends to visit, shall be cared for by the respective Superintendents.

SEC. 2. There shall be no restriction as to age. The regular course shall be five years; but the Board in its discretion may in particular cases order the retention or discharge of any pupil. No pupil shall be discharged except upon the order of the Board.

SEC. 3. The County Judges shall select the pupils apportionment having been made by the Board of Education as provided for in the case of boarding schools. Regard shall be had in selections to the most needy, and more than one pupil may be sent from the same family.

SEC. 4. Each Sheriff shall collect all pupils and take them in one trip to the proper school. He shall be allowed $2.00 per day and actual necessary expenses, to be paid out of the respective County Treasuries upon properly certified accounts.

SEC. 5. The Superintendents of orphan schools shall give a similar bond and shall report in like manner to the Board as prescribed in this act for Superintendents of boarding schools.

This act shall take effect from and after its passage and approval, and all other acts and parts of acts on the subject of schools are hereby repealed.

APPROVED, October 31, 1890.

W. N. JONES,
P. C. C. N.

BILL LXII.

An Act to punish Official Corruption and the Bribery of Voters.

Be it enacted by the General Council of the Choctaw Nation assembled.

SECTION 1. Any Choctaw citizen holding any office of honor, trust or profit, under the Choctaw government, and any witness or juror in any Choctaw courts who shall corruptly take or accept any money, valuable thing or consideration whatever, either before or after such officer, witness or juror has qualified, offered him or her by any other person with intent to influence the official action or duty of such officer, witness or juror, shall be deemed guilty of a felony, and upon indictment and conviction thereof, shall be punished by a fine of not less than one hundred dollars, and in default of the payment of such fine for one day, shall receive not less than thirty-nine (39) nor more than one hundred (100) lashes well laid on the bare back.

SEC. 2. Any person who shall corruptly offer, or attempt to offer to any qualified voter of the Choctaw Nation at any general or special election held under the Choctaw laws, any intoxicating liquor, money or valuable thing whatever, as a consideration for the suffrage of said voter, or with intent to influence said voter, as to his vote, or to subvert his free choice, shall be deemed guilty of a felony, and upon indictment and conviction, shall be punished as provided in section 1 of this act.

This act shall take effect from and after its passage and approval.

APPROVED, November 3, 1890.

W. N. JONES, P. C. C. N.

BILL LXIII.

An Act to facilitate the Detection of Larceny of Cattle in the Choctaw Nation.

Be it enacted by the General Council of the Choctaw Nation assembled, That every butcher doing business in this Nation shall keep a written record of the marks and brands of all cattle and hogs purchased for slaughter and from whom purchased; at the end of each month he shall file the same with the Clerk of the County Court in the county in which such butcher does business.

SEC. 2. It shall be the duty of each County Clerk to safely preserve such record so filed and to freely permit the public to inspect the same.

SEC. 3. The violation of any of the provisions of this act shall constitute a misdemeanor, and shall be punished by a fine of not less than $5 nor more than $25. In case the offender be a non-citizen his license as butcher permit shall be revoked.

SEC. 4. This act shall take effect from and after its passage and approval.

APPROVED November 13, 1890.

W. N. JONES, P. C. C. N.

CHAHTA OKLA

I NAN ULHPIESA,

NAN APESA ITTUNAHA CHITO YUT

1886 Heket 1890,

—ONT AI ULHEHE—

NAN ULHPISA IKBI TOK, AI̲ TOKOWA.

1890.
Hattak upi Aiachuffa Holisso ai I̲ Chu̲le,
ATOKA, I. T.

INTEX,

CHAHTA OKLA

—I NAN ULHPISA—

1886 MICHA 1890 ONT AIULHEHE.

———o———

BILL I.

Nan it hana i Superintendent" isht imvulhtoba ya ishaleh chit ibufokki Nan Uhlpesa,

Chahta Okla Nan vpesa ittanaha Chito ittafamat chiya ka yakohmit Ulhpesashke Nan ithana i "Superintendent" isht imvlhtoba yat afammi achaffa ka tali holisso talhepa ushta hashki, achi ilappat lhupulli hyat aiahlit hvlittopashki.

October 12, 1886 Aiokpachi,

T, McKINNEY,
Chahta Okla I miko chito.

BILL II.

Oka hawashko chahta bea achi keyukmat peh nana hosh hataka inlachit haksschi hvkma nana hinla ikikbo kachi nan vlhpesa. Chata okla nan vpesa ittanaha chito ittafamat chiya ka yakahmit vhlpesashke, hatak kana hosh aka hawashko chahta bea achi keyeokmat nana inla kat hat oka haksecha henla ho ikbit ahanta ka ilappat imoktabelishki. Nana yamma chiyohmi ka nan vlhtoka yat oupanit kancha he vt imai vlhpiesa yamohmikma yamma isht aya hatuk okma ikbi okma nana hatuk ok-mat oka homi yatuk akinli ho aiittilauuit na palammi onnotolashki achi ilappat lhopulli hayat aiahlit holittopashki.

October 18, 1886 Aiokpachi.

T. McKINNEY,
Chata okla i miko chito.

BILL III.

County ut Jackson honchifohosh tobo nan ulhpesa.

Chahta okla nan upesa ittanaha chito ittafumat chiya ka yakohmit ulhpesashki, Kaunti achaffa kat Kaunti tuchena Kiamitia micha Okchamali Atoka Kaunti aiena ka atoshafa hosh Jackson Kaunti hohchifo hosh tobat ibafokkashki, yohmi kat yakni hlafa isht ottayani kat yakohmashki. Lhabeta yat Bok homma asitili fehma hikiyat ia hosh abayahanchit lhabeta Bok aiitaafama fehna yako alayohmik mat Muddy Boggy yako abayachit iya hosh Thompson Wesley i hina akocha out iakmat Atoka i chukka atok lossa apotaka talaya ka ona yohmi mat anoti hina himona Hettie Carnes i chukka ont ia ka abayachit aya hosh Clear Boggy a onashki. Yohmi mat Caddo hena a fokkat aya hosh Wilson Jones i nan uhlp oba aiimpa holehta ya onashki, yohmikmat holehta yamma hashi akochaka imma bachaya kako abayachit asa hosh Boggy Depot hina sipokni ya onashki, yohmikmat hena yamma fokkat aya hosh Jack Risner i chukka yat isht ulhpisa (250) Kaunti a pit an okaka ho talayashki yahmik mat Phelin Wahli i Bok ushi ya abyachit okchamali Boka onashki, yohmik mat Okchamali ya afokkat ia hosh Bok homma ya onashki, yohmik mat Bok humma ya fokkat ia hosh Lhabeta asitili ka ona cha ahikiat ia amona tuka alashki.

October 26, 1886 Aiokpachi.

T. McKINNEY,
Miko Chito.

BILL IV.

Himak ma anoti "Inspector" tuklo ka atukola chi nan ulhpesa.

SECTION 1- Chahta okla nan upesa ettanaha chito ittafamat chiya Ka yakoohmit uhlpasa shki. Miko chito ut himakma In-

spector tuklo ka atokoli heat imaiachlpeisa, yohmi kat St. Louis and San Frncisco Tali hina atoksali kat achaffa kat Ft. Smith, Arkansas ako hikiyat Toshkaomma C. N. a alakma anoti achaffa kat Tushkahoma, C. N. hikiyat Bok Homma ya onashki, yohmi kat "Inspector" ahachi ilappat Choctaw Nation Citizen ashki.

SEC. 2. Ont achakaya ka yakohmashki "Inspector" ahan chi ilappat Nan ulhepesa October 1883 toba tokako aieyakaykaya hosh ulhtokashki.

SEC. 3. Ont achakaya ka yakohmashki, yohmi ka "Inspector" Non ulhtoka eishi yammat November 6, 1883, Nan ulhepsa aiyakkaiat uhltoka tok at M., K. & T. tali hina micha afelamoli putta chatta yakni bachohat maya kak inli eyeshashki, yohmikma yakohmashki achi ilappat lhupulli hayat ayahlit holittopashki.

October 22, 1886.

T. McKINNEY,
Miko Chito.

BILL V.

Jackson County ut aboha Nakfish achaffa kat emulhttoka he nan uhlpesa.

Chahta okla nan upesa ittanaha chito ittafamat chiya ka yakohmit uhlpesashki, himaka pelah hokano Jackson County okat aboha nakfish achffa kat fot I kania alheha hatukmat atokoli ho imayalhtoka heyokat imuiulhpiesa achi ilappat lhupulli haya aialhit hollittopashki.

October 29, 1886 Aiokpachi.

T. McKINNEY,
Miko Chito.

BILL VI.

Senatorial "District" Pushmataha achi Nan uhlpesa.

Chahta Okla nan upesa ittanaha Chito ittafamat chiya ka yakohmit Uhlpesashki, yohmikat ilappat lhopulli hayat himak pelah ha holitt opashki okchamamall Kaunty micha Jackson

Kaunti ittatuklo kat Senator ʋt achaffa hosh nan ʋpesa ittanaha chito ya imayashki.

Ont achakaya ka yakoamishki achi ilappat lhupulli hayat August amona 1888 aiʋhlit iya ka holittopashki.

October 29, 1886, Aiokpachi.

T. McKINNEY,
Miko Chito.

BILL VII.

District ont atuchena ya anumpa ettolapoutta kat akaniohma he Nan ʋlhpesa.

Chahta Okla nan ʋpesa ittanaha chito cahhta yakni aiittafamat cheya ka yakohmit ʋlhpesashki anumpa Nana ho isht aionʋttola yohkia anumpa onottola yat Okchamali Kaunti Koat micha Atoka Kaunti micha Kiamitia Kaunti, Jack Fork Kaunti aiena ka ahanta atuk ohkia, anumpa onnotola micha nana unanoli aiena kat Jackson Kaunti anokakayoaahanta hatuk mat Jackson Kaunti Koat ako pet afoyoka shki. Yohmikma anumpa ettola holisso poyutta ka Jackson Kaunti I Kaunti Judge atukmat Kaunti ahanchi kash i holissochi ya imashki. Yohmi kia anumpa onottola micha nana imanoli aiena kat Jackson Kaunti Anokaka ahanta ho keyu hok mono anumpa ettola yat yammak inli ho ettoyula tukmat nana ka isht anokfillih shki. Achi ilappat lhupulli hayat February 1, 1887 aiʋlhlhit ia ka holittopashki.

October 27, 1886 Aiokpachi.

T. McKINNEY,
Miko chito.

BILL VIII.

Chahta Okla nan ʋpesa ittanaha chito chahta yakni aiittafamat cheya ka yakohmit ʋlhpesashki.

Okchamali Kaunti ʋt Shalif apelachi yat imoshtashki Atoka, Kiamitia, Jocks Fork micha Jackson Kaunti aiena dat Shalif ʋpelachi yat imushta banshki. Yohmikma nan ʋlhpesa ilppa anotakat ulhtoka tuk okato isht imulhtoba yat $50.00 Tali holisso pokoli tahlapi hasoh Nation Treasury akocha hosh imuhltobashki Shalif moma ishahli ut certificate atukma emashki achi ilappat lhupulli hayat February 1, 1887 aiulhlit ia ka holitopashke anumpa Bohli, Billy Williams.

October 30, 1885 Aiokpochi.

T. McKINNEY,
Chahta Okla I miko Chito.

BILL IX.

District ont atucklhna ya Jurors ut kanohma chi Nan Ulhpesa.

Chahta okla nan upesa ittanaha chito ittafamat chiya ka yakohmit ulhpesashki.

Circuit Court, Third Judicial District, aiittafama August amona 1887 micha yamma aiuhlit ia ka Jury ut yakohmashke. Okchamli kaunti ut Jury imontochenashke. Atoka yut Jury imontochena; Jack's Fork ut imontachena; Kiamitia ut Jury imontochena; Jackson kaunti ut Jury imontuchenashki.

Ont achakaya ka yakomit ulhpesashki, Yakomashki achi ilappat lhupulli haya nan ulhpesa ilappak oka akashapa kaniohmi ka ai isanali hokato Akshashki yohmek ma elappat lhopulli hayat March 1, 1887, aiahlit ia ka aiahlit holittopashke.

October 30th, 1886, ai okpachi.

THOMPSON McKINNEY,
Miko Chito.

BILL X.

Circuit Court Pushmataba District, Choctaw Nation, ahikia chatuk ut Atoka ya akanalichit Jackson Kaunti yako pit hikia chi nan ulhpesa.

Chahta okla nan upesa ittanaba Chito Chahta yakni aiittafamat chiya ka yakohmit ulhpesashki Circuit Court Pushmataba.

District ut Tiak Heli Jackson kaunti ahekia chatuk ut kanallit Tiak Heli Jackson kaunti ako February, 1887, aiulhit micha himak pela hokano Pushmataha District Circuit Court ʋt Tiak Hili Jackson kaunti, C. N. Ako ahikkiashki, achi ilappat lhupulli hayat aialhit holittopashki.

Nov. 1, 1886, aiokpachi.

THOMPSON McKINNEY,
Miko Chito.

BILL XI.

Jackson Kaunti I Shalif ʋt ʋlhtoka cha Pushmataha District Circuit Court atukma nana isht ahanta chi nan ʋlhpesa.

Yohmi ka Jackson kaunti I Shalif atukmat ʋlhtokat im ʋlhtayaha cha Pushmataha District Circuit Court "atukma nan isht ahanta chikat Shalif tekba yatuka Receipt," micha nan isht aiahanta holisso micha Hattak ʋbi ittialla he aiʋlhpiesa moyoma kat ebbak afoyokashki. Nan ʋlhpesa nana hosh yakohmashki achi ilappa ai isanali putta kat akshoshki yohmi na yakohmashki achi ilappat lhuppuli hayat February 1, 1887, aiahlit ia ka holittopashki.

Nov. 1, 1886, aiokpachi.

THOMPSON McKINNEY,
Miko Chito.

BILL XII.

Chahta okla i nan ʋpesa ittanaha chito ittafamat chiya ka yakohmit ʋlhpesashke,

SECTION 1. Himak pela hokano Chahta yakni ilappa aiibaholhtina keyu hosh Chahta ebaholhtina bannat nan ʋpesa ya anumpa nan asilhha ibohli kat Chahta issish kashapa isht untuchena ho ishikat nan anoa aiʋlhpiesa ho isht ilaiatokoli hokmakashki.

SEC. 2. Achakaya ka yakohmit ʋlhpesashke, Chahta yakni ilappa ebaholhtina he ahnit anumpa nan asilhha bohli putta kat nahullo micha Chahta issish itti balhto ho ilaieishi kat ilai tokoli hokmakashki.

SEC. 3. Achakaya ka yakohmit ʋlhpesashki, Kana Hohkia nan ʋlhpesa kobaffi anumpa ʋlhtokowa onotola hokato Chahta Yakni ilappa aiibaholhtina ik tobokashki.

SEC. 4. Achakaya ka yakohmit vlhpesashki, Chahta yakni ilappa ibaholhtinat imvlhtaba yosh Nation ilappa maya kano nan vlhpesa ilappat ikataklammicho kashki.

SEC. 5. Achakayv ka yakohmit vlhpesashki, Nan vlhpesa ilappat lhopulli hayat aiahlit holittopashki.

THOMPSON McKINNEY,
Miko Chito.

BILL XIII.

Ranger isht imvlhtoba yat Tali holisso pokoli Tahlapi hachi nan vlhpesa.

Chahta okla I nan vpesa ittanaha chito ittafamat chiya ka yakohmit vlhpesashki, Chahta yakni anokaka Kaunti I Ranger hoohlit aiasha kat isht imvlhtoba yat nan vlhpesa yat imissa yatok a ishikmak anoti Tali holisso pokoli talhapi hosh Nation i Tali holisso Sholi ya ai imvlhtobashki Yamohma chika Kaunti i holissochi atukmat Satifeket atukma ima ho isht imvlhtoba yat hashi tuchena aiv okak ma imvlhtobashki nan vlhpesa ilappat`lhopulli hayat aiahlit holittopashki.

Nov. 5, 1886, aiokpachi.

THOMPSON McKINNEY.

BILL XIV.

Chahta okla I nan vpesa ittanaha Chito Chahta yakni aiittafamat chiya ka yakohmit vlhpesashke.

Chata yakni ilappa ibah hohltina keyu hosh ittatoba I permit keyukmat pamit kaniohmi hohkia anotakat Nation ilappa aiatta keyukmat nana toksali hosh ahanta chi kat ilap nan isht ai okpa chi kat ilap aivtta chokka achuffa ka misha keyu kashki, ittatoba yosh Tamaha keyukmat Tamaha ushi yo ahanto chikat aiittatoba chokka atalaya chika Tamvha chokka atalaya aivlhpesa tuklo hokano misha keyokashki.

SEC. 2. Chahta yakni ilappa ibah ohltina keyo hosh aivtta chokka keyukmot chokka haniohmi hohkia italayat inla ipota he ahmi, keyukmat ipota tuk ukma nana hokmat nan vlhpesa ilappat lhopulli tuka nitak pokoli hanali aiittintakla ka kan-chashki. Yamohmi keyukma Chahta yakni ibaholhtina keyo nan immi isht tahpalat kancha he aiimma Oct. 30, 1877. Nan ʋlhpisa toba tok nana amia kako isht imalhekashki.

Sec. 3. Holehta chito keyukmat Hohleta nana hohkia Chahta yakni ilappa ibaholhtina keyo ho immi hokato nan ʋlhpesa ilappat lhupulli tuk a nitak pokoli Hanali aiittintakla ka Chahta yakni ilappa ebaholhtina yo ikanchashki. Yamohmi keyukma kaunti nana ho Holehta ahanchi kash atalaya hokma kaunti yamma i Shalif ʋt kanalli chaski.

Keyukmat Holetah yamma tiwi na citizen putta kako nan isht imai ʋlhpiesa yo tobashki.

Sec. 4. Nan ʋlhpesa ilappat Section amona nana amia ka Chahta ibaholhtina keyo kat ikalhho hokmat nan ikalho isht ʋlhpesa cha I permit atukmat ikania shki. Yohmi cha Intruder, isht ʋlhpesa na kanalla he a miko chito ʋt mihashki. Nan ʋlhpesa ilappat lhopulli hayat ai alhit holittopshki.

Oct. 28, 1887, aiokpachi.

THOMPSON McKINNEY,
Miko Chito.

BILL XV.

Chahta yakni ilappa i nan ʋlhtoka Intruders aiimma atoksali yat akaniohma he otanichi nan ʋlhpesa.

Chahta okla i nan ʋpesa ittanaha chito ittafamat chiya ka yakohmit ʋlhpesashki.

BILL XVI.

Tali Holisso Sholi I holissochi nan isht Aiʋtta otanichi nan Ʋlhpesa.

Chahta okla I nan ʋpesa ittanaha chito ittafamat chiya yakohmit ʋlhpesashki.

Chahta okla I Tali Hollisso sholi I holissochi yat nan ʋlhpesa ilappa Auet iakaya kako ai eyakaya keyo hokato iskali isht hoyo nana kia ikba hiat imaeʋlhpiesa keyo kashki.

Sec. 2. Achakaya ka yakomit vlhpesashki, "Nation" I Tali holisso Sholi I holissochi yat imaiʋlhpiesa cha hashi ont

Atuchena ia Amona ka Nation" illappa Anokaka nan ulhtoka hiohli putta ka isht imulhtoba yat nan ulhpesa hosh amia ho Nation I tali holisso sholi ako ai imulht-oba hokma iskali isht hoyo (Wallent) a ikbit hashi tuchena isht imulht-oba he ai ulhpesa ka imashki. Ulhti micha Nation" I nan ulhtoka Aiena hokano Tali holisso sholi I holissochi yat iskali isht hoyo a Apissalichit Aiimmi hatuka pit imashki, Nan ulhtoka inla putta isht imulhtoba Yokano Kaunti Aiokali I Judge. Ako pit ima na Nan vlhpesa ilappat ameha kako iakaya hosh Nan ulhtoka Ai okali ka imashki Nation I holissochi chito ut imaiulhpiesa cha kana ho nan isht ulhtoka ima tuk micha nitak holhtina ai ena ka Taliholisso sholi I holisso chi ya im an oachi cha ittaba eisha shki.

Circuit Court ai okali I shalif ut I "Deputy" Shalif hoh chito Micha nitak nana ho At okali tuk putta kat Tali holisso Sholi I hollissochi ya imann-woachashki.

SEC. 3. Achakaya ka yakohmit ulhpesashki. Nan-ulht oka nana hohkia Okla moma imiskali ittahobbi, Keyukmat I Superintendent okma nana hokmat hashi Achaffa ont taha aiokali ka kani ohmi hosh iskali yat at toba tuka Tali holisso Shali a hollissochi ya im otanicha shki, yohmikma Tali holisso sholi I holissochi ut yammako Ai eakaya hosh nan ulhtoka ahan chi kash isht imvlhtoba chika iskali isht hoyo ya imashki.

SEC. 4. Achakaya ka yakomit ulhpesa shki, Nation ilappa I Kot putta imahl-uka yat "Nation" I Tali holisso sholi ya akucha hosh ulhtoba chika nan ulhpesa yat imissa putta ka Judge Akosh Alni ho Kot I holissochi akosh atahli cha (seal). Atukma lapa-l ech icha Ahl-uka ahanchi kash nan ulhpesa eana ho aniotaka ka otanichi hosh kot ut tishili tok a nitak achaffa aiitint-akla ho Tali Holiss sholi I holissochi ya pit ipelashki.

SEC. 5. Achakaya ka yakohmit ulhpesashki. Nan ulhpesa ilappat Feb. 1, 1888, hikiyat iya ka Aialhit holittopaski.

November 7, 1887, Aiokpachi.

T. McKINNEY,

Miko Chito.

BILL XVII.

Tali Fabassa hoiehta micha holehta chito putta Aiimma nan ulhpesa ya ibafokki nan ulhpesa.

Chahta okla I nan upesa ittanaha chito itt afamat chiya ka yakohmit ulhpesashki Hatak kana hohkia "citizen" ohkia I hohlehta chito ya inlu immi ya ittitikilicha hi at im ai ulhpiesa keyo kashki, holehta Ahanchi kash putta kat ittinlakla yat patha kat iyi pokoli tuklo ola keyo kashki. Nan uhlpisa ilappa kobaffi putta ka Kaunti "Judge" ut ay ohma hiat im ai ulhpiesa cha Shalif a at-ohno na chalit kenahlechi na aiittan-owa he putta kat haya-kashki.

Nan ulhpesa ilappat lhopulli hay at Ai alhit holitt opashki.

November 8, 1887, Aiokpachi.

THOMPSON McKINNEY,
Miko Chito.

BILL XVIII.

Nan ulhtoka kuchi ai imma otanchi nan ulhpesa.

SECTION 1. Chahta okla I nan upesa ittanhaha chito itta-famat chiya ka yakohmit ulhpesashki. Chahta yakni ilappa I "citizen kanimma hohkia tuche na ka ona hokmat Nation," key-ukmat ulhta i nan ulhtoka kanimma hohkia Miko Chito akkeyo hokma nan ulhtoka hekeyat nana ikaiulhpeso hokma Miko Chito ya im otanichashki, yohmi cha yammak inli ho chohmechi hosh Miko Chito yat ikaiulhpeso hokma nan upesa ya imotanichashki yohmikmat yammak inli ohmi ka holissochi chito I holisso af okkashki.

SEC. 2. Anumpa onichi ahanchi kash o chohmi kat "Nation ilappa I Judge" kanimma ho ammpa kallo aiishi cha nana ho isht ikaiulhpeso hatukma otanichashki, micha nan an-oli achukma tuklo hosh im aien ashki. Miko Chito yat imaiulh-piesa cha ilappa aiimma kat isht ai ulhpiesa chika ammpa kallo nana hohkia ono cha hia nan ulhpesa ilappat imisashki.

SEC. 3. Anumpa isht ai onatola ahanchi kash Miko Chito yat af analechi cha nan ulhtoka ikkucho hokma okla putta kia isht ataklama hinla ahni hokmat uitak nana ho kanimma aiitafama chika nitak pokoli hosh takli moma ho im anoachashki. Yohmi cha nana kaniohmi ho nan ulhtoka hekeya tuk ut ik kucho ka hinla ahni hokmat ilotanichashki. Yohmi kia nan ulhtoka ahanchi kash nan isht aiikashofa he aiulhpesa ka ilotanichi keyo hosh ikhaya-kotuk okma antta hetuka chohmi ho Miko Chito yat yammak atuka afanalicha-shki yohmi cha Miko Chito yat ittichapa in an anoli ya imahaponaklochkma ulhtoka hikiya heat aiulhpesa keyo ahani hokmat kuchashki. Yohmi kia nan ulhpesa yosh amia hokiyo hokano Miko Chito yat nan alhtoka nana kia ikkucho kashki.

SEC. 4. Anumpa nana hohkia ilappako anotaka hosh ittola hokma Miko Chito yat anumpa nana micha nan annowa yohmikmat ilap ut nana ho aiimanukfila aiena kat amominchi hosh Holissochi chito ya pit ema na yammak atuk ma holisso putta ka nan upesa ittafamat chiyakma aboha nakfish im anumpa eshi ya ibbak fokashki.

SEC. 5. Nan ulhtoka yat kucha he ai ulhpesa ka aboha nakfish nan apesa yat ahni hokmat nan ulhtoka kuchi anumpa ha atahli cha aboha Akni ya pit imashki, yohmicha aboha nakfish ut chikosi kat kaniohmi kako ai ulhpesa hinla hokma nan ulhtoka kuchi aiimma isht asha chika atokolashki yohmikmat anumpa onnotola yatuk ut nitak nana ho haiaka chika imupesa cha isht im an owa holisso atahli cha aboha akni I Miko ilap hoh chifo ya takalichi na achakaya ka holissochi chito yat ilap hoh chifo ya takilichi cha, nan ulhtoka kuchi banna anumpa hash holba yo aiinichi cha anumpa onotola yatuk ut nitak ulhpesa tuka hayaka cha anumpa isht onotola kat anumpa afalama ikbashki. Nan isht imanowa ahanchi kash anumpa onotola atuka ilap fehma isht imanowa chashki yohmi kia anumpa onotola yatuk ut ikhaiyako hokmano nan isht imanowa micha nan ulhtoka kuchi anumpa hatuka hobachit ikbi cha anumpa onotola yammat aiutta ya kanah hat afammi auahanali ka ont iya kat anta hokma imashki.

SEC. 6. Nan ulhpesa ilappa alhecha chikat holisso shali akosh apelachi kanohmi ai ena hosh ulhpesa ka aboha akni I Miko akosh ahni hokma nan ulhtoka kuchi I Kot yammat nana ho abanna ka moma atoksalashki. Holisso shali apelachi ahanchi kash abanna keyo ahni hokmat aboha akni I Miko yat kuch.

ashki, yohmi cha nan ʋlhtoka kuchi kot chi̱ya ka aboha akni akosh imaiʋlh piesa cha nan isht aia̱lhi-cha chi̱ ka̱ ilaieshashki. Micha anumpa ittola tuka̱ isht ai opi ka̱ ittiba anukfiillashki. Yohmi akinli kia anumpa onotola tuk ʋt ikhaiako, keyukmat haiaka hohkia anumpa afalama ikba hikiyo hokma aboha akni ʋt at-oksalashki.

SEC. 7. Anumpa itto̱la tuka̱ isht wakaya keyo ki̱sha ka aboha akni I̱ Mi̱ko yat nan isht asha chi̱ ka̱ anumpa kallo onuchashki. Yohmikma aboha akni I̱ Mi̱ko ya̱ holissochi yat anumpa kallo anuchashki yohmikma anumpa ittola yatukma af analichit, micha nan ʋlhpesa. Nan anowa aiena kako iyakka̱ya hosh nan ʋlhtoka kuchi ai imnna ka isht at-oksalashki. Okla moma kat isht imaiʋlhpiesa hinla ahni hokmat anumpa ittola tuka̱ nitak inla ho isht asha hiat imaiʋlhpiesashki. Yohmi cha nan ʋlhpesa hosa amia hokma anumpa ittola ilappa̱ aiimma ka̱ nana ponaklo putta kat imaiʋlhpiesacha ponaklashki, yohmi kat kot inla nana ponaklo chatuka̱ aiittilaiwichi hosh ponaka̱k-la hiat imaiʋlhpiesashki yohmi hokano yohmi aknili kia fot i̱kania putta kat anumpa ittola nana hatukma yammak inli kat nan ʋlhtoka kuchi I̱ kot ahanchi kash afokkashki.

SEC. 8. Nan ʋlhtoka kuchi anumpa hat Mi̱ko Chito ako isht ai onotola hokma Mi̱ko Chito hiki̱ya tuk ʋt yikopa na kot moma i̱shahli I̱ "Judge" kanimma hosh ʋlhto̱bat ashashki.

SEC. 9. Nan ʋlhtoka kuchi kot ʋt nana isht asha tuk putta ka aboha akni I̱ holissochi yat hobachit ishi cha nitak himmak apesa he mako̱ holissochito nan isht ai ʋtta ya̱ afokkashki. Nan ʋlhpesa ilappat lhopulli hay at ai a̱lhit holitt opashki.

November 8, 1887, Aiokpachi.

THOMPSON McKINNEY,

Mi̱ko Chito.

BILL XIX.

Chahta Citizen achaffakma atampa hokma nana hohkia Citizen keyo ka̱ nan ʋlhpoba apesachi iktohno ka chi nan ʋlhpesa.

Chahta Okla I̱nan ʋpesa ittana-ha chito ittafamat chiya ka yakohmit ʋlhpesashki. Citizen achaffa hokma kanohmi hokma nana hohkia. Citizen keyo achiffa hohhma atampa hakma nana hohkia wak, Issoba haksobish falaya, chukfi issi Kosoma, shukha micha nan ulhpoba nana hoh kia apisachi tohna hiat imaiulhpisa keyo kashki, micha "Nation" anokaka ilappa nan ulhpoba hayaka asha nana hohkia hoyo, ittahobi, akanimma hohkia iktohno kashki, Holhta yo apitat epeta chi hokmano nan ulhpesa ilappat imoktabli keyo kashki. Hatak achaffa keyumat hatak kanuhmi nana hohkia nan ulhpesa ilappa Kobaffi hokma Circuit Court" itikba anumpa isht aaionotala cha ulhtoba onnot, tola kat Tali holisso Talhepa Tuklo pokoli Talhapi ka ola keyukmat Tali holisso Talhepa Talhapi kano misha keyo hosh ulhtoba onotolashki, isht ulhtoba ahanchi kash iklanna kat Nation aiimma i Tali holsso sholi ako imiashki yohmikma iklanna kat nan anoli tuk ako imashki achakaya ka yakohmit ulhpesa ashki. Nan ulhpiesa ilappa auet iakaya ka nan ulhpesa, Keyukmat nan ulhpesa akashapa nana hohkia aiisanali hokmat akshona nan ulhpesa ilappat lhopulli hayat ai aialhit holittopashki. Nov. 9, 1887. THOMPSON McKINNEY, Miko Chito.

BILL XX.

Tali holisso sholi isht apelachi Aiimma nan ulhpesa.

Chahta Okla I nan upesa ittanaha chito ittafamat chiya ka yakohmit ulhpesashki Tali holisso Talhepa ushta hosh afammi achaffa aiokaikma Tali holisso sholi ut nan ulhtokat hikiyat nana isht elapelacha chi ka ittolashki Issoba obinili hochito ut Tali holisso sholi atonit abinachit impat maya chika isht ulhtoba-shiki. Yohmi hoka Taliholisso shol ut afammi achaffa aiokalikma isht ulhtoba ahanchi kash kaniuhm ho isht elapelachi tuk ut nan ut nan upesa ya imotanihichashki nan ulhpesa ilappat lhopulli hokma ashalika miko chito yat ai akaya hosh Tali holissoo sholi ut kana hachi ka meha ho Issoba obinnili chito tuklo ka atokoli na Tali holisso Sholi amia kako anotaka hosh toksalashki Issoba obinili chito tikba ulhtoka yatuka ittauklo keyukmat kanimapo ka Tali holisso sholi ut imulhtoka banna keyo hokma isht ulhtoko ya akshochashki nan ulhpesa ilappat lhopulli hayat ai alhit holittopashki.

November 9, 1887 Aiokpachi.

THOMPSON McKINNEY, Miko chito.

BILL XXI.

Uba anumpa ishi Aiimma 1866 Treaty toba tok apoksiachi nan ʋlhpesa.

Chahta okla I nan ʋpesa ittanaho chito ittafamat chiya ka yakohmit ʋlhpesashki.

Chahta, Chikasha ittatuklo iyakni halalli aiimma isht annowa Treaty, Article 11, 1866, toba tok ʋt ik alho ma. Ahalaya tuk micha anotaka tuk putta kat aienat ikalhoshki. Yohmi hoka Treaty micha Article holisso tokahhanchi kash nana amia kat akshashki. Yohmikma ʋba anumpa eshi, micha hatak kashkoa nana hohkia yammat amia hokano isht ai alhi ʋt ikimikshoshki. Nan ʋlhpesa ilappat lhopulli hayat, ai alhit holittopashki.

Nov. 9, 1887, aiokpachi.

THOMPSON McKINNEY,
Miko Chito.

BILL XXII.

Hashok bashli aiimma Nov. 1, 1882, nan ʋlhpesa toba tok akalli nan ʋlhpesa.

Chahta okla I nan ʋpesa ittanaha chito ittafamat chiya ka yakohmit ʋlhpesashki.

November 1, 1882, kash nan ʋlhpesa tok ʋt citizen keyo micha Permit attobbi putta ka hashok bashlit Pini apitat kanimma akancha he imissa yatuk ʋt akshashki, himakma yakohmashki. Citizen keyo micha Permit attobi putta kat hashok basha ya ilap abanna illa kat citizen o imaiishi hashkik. Nan ʋlhpesa ilappa kobaffi putta kat Nation ilappa kuchashke.

Nan ʋlhpesa ilappat lhopulli hayat aiahlit holittopashki.

November 10, 1887, aiokpachi.

THOMPSON McKINNEY,
Miko Chito.

BILL XXIII.

Okla putta imaboha aiimma nan ʋlhpesa.

Chahta okla I nan ʋpesa ittanaha chito ittafamat chiya ka

yakohmit ulhpesashki. Hatak kana hohkia Nation ilappa an-okaka okla putta im aboha ya kanimihchit ai opanichi, hokma ulhti yamma I chuli hochito akosh anumpa onuchi na ulhtoba anotola kat Tali holisso pokoli talhapi ka ola keyokmot Talhepa achaffa ka misha keyo kashki, micha aboha ahanchi kash kanimihchi hosh apanichi tuk mat yamma ai okali ka atobbashki yohmi cha nana aiopanichi tuk micha ulhtoba onnutola tuk putta kat Atobba hikiyo hokma innali bieka ho fama pokoli Talhapi ka ola keyokmat Talhepa achaffa hokano misha keyo hosh onnotolashki. Nan ulhpesa ilappat lhopulli hayat aialhit holittopashke.

November 10, 1887, aiokpachi.

THOMPSON McKINNEY,

Miko Chito.

BILL XXIV.

Ittihalalli aiimma November 9, 1875, nan ulhpesa toba tuka akalli nan ulhpesa.

Chahta okla I nan upesa ittanaha chito ittafamat chiya ka yakohmit ulhpesashki, Nahullo yat Chahta ahoyo ittihalalli aiimma November 9, 1875, kash nan ulhpesa toba tok ut yakohmi hosh alhkatashki. Kaunti iholissochi illa hosh ittihalalli imissa holisso ha imatahlashki. Yohmikma nahullo yat Tuli holiso pokule tuklo, akuchcha Talhapi ho Atobbi chatuk aibafoka na Tali holisso Talhepa achaffa ho at obbashki. Yokmikma kaunti I holissochi ut ittahalalli imissaholisso kuchi micha iskali ya ulhtoba tok putta ishi kat isht imulhtoba yat Tali holisso tuklo 50-00 hashki, inla kano County I Tuli holiso shole ako ibbak fokkashke November 9, 1875. Nan ulhpesa yat holitopashki. Nan ulhpesa ilappat lhopulli hayat ai alhit holittopashki.

Nov. 10, 1887, aiokpachi.

THOMPSON McKINNEY,

Miko Chito.

BILL XXV.

Chike ka̱ Chahta Okla i̱ nan vlhpisa ittibafokkit holisso ikbe tok yammak osh holisso vlhtaha yammak fihna akinle hosh nan vlhpisa ai a̱lhe atok acchit nan vlhpisa ikbi.

Yakohmishke, nan apisa yvt Nofimba 3rd, 1885, ash nan vlhpisa ikbit holitoblechi tok Chahta Okla i̱ nan vlhpisa yvt holesso toba he a̱ apesa micha Mi̱ko Chito Holessochi chito Hopaie chito aina kak osh Kommitte yosh nan vlhpisa ya̱ ittibafokkit tosholet micha holisso ikbi micha nan ittim apisa ittimatahle ka̱ ai i̱ nutaka hosh na̱ tuksale ha̱ ai a̱lha chi̱ ka̱ Ban aina ka̱ ittimatahleshke.

Atuko̱ yakomishke Kommitte achi kash micha nan ittim apisa achi kash ai ittimatahle ka̱ na̱ tovsale vlhtaha tuka̱ aiokpachit ishi tok, isht imvlthtoba chi ka̱ Satifikit ima tok na toksale hvt momat vlhtobat-toba tok oke, yammohme hoka; auit iyaka̱ya kak osh holesso tohomba tuka̱ nan vlhpisa makashke.

Chahta Okla Nan apisa ittanaha chito ittafamat cheya ka̱ yakohmit vlhpisashke yohmi kvt holesso toba tok ahanchi kash yammak fihna akinle ka̱ Chahta Okla i̱ nan vlhpisa yat, moyomat atoyokka tok yohmi batuko̱ yammako̱ okla imatiyat holittablashke.

Nan vlhpisa ilappat lhupulle ma kinle hosh ai alhit holittopat ittoyolashke.

Aiokpache Aktoba 30, 1888.

B. F. SMALLWOOD,
Chahta Okla I̱ Mi̱ko Chito.

BILL XXVI.

Nan vlhtuka vlhiba hvt Koniohme kako̱ anumpa kallo im vlhtaha he nan vlhpisa.

Section 1. Chahta Okla nan apesa ittanahat cheya ka̱ yakohmet vlhpesashke. Yohme kvt Vlhtih micha Kaunte i̱ nan vlhtuka vlhiba ha̱ Chach chito yat satifikit ima tuk a̱ Aktoba mittak vmmona hokmako anumpa kollo im vlhtaha cha ilapo atoksala he ai vlhpeyesa vlhtuka tuk aioka kat nana akaniohme na kuchche keyuo hokma tuksahanle na afomme tuklashke.

SEC. 2. Ont achukaya ka yakomet ulhpesashke, abohaknih micha abohanakfish ai ittapehat nan ulhtuka atokole ulhiha micha abohakne at im aiokpanche ho miko chito ut nan ulhtuka atokule tuk ulhiha aina kut Nofimba nittak ummona, kako annumpa kallo im ulhtuha cha, nan toksale isht ai atta he im ai ulhpiesa tuk ut toksalet isht mahayashke.

SEC. 3. Ont achakaya ka yauohmet ulhpesashke, Okla hosh atokule tuko nan ulhtuka ulhiha hovoto himak pila Aktoba nittak ummona 1890. Ont imai ulhashke, yohmikma nan apesa kiyoumat Miko Chito osh atokole tuk ulhiha hut Nofimba nittak ummona 1890, kako ont im ai ulh-lhashke.

SEC. 4. Ont achakaya ka yakohmet ulhpesashke nan ulhpesa ilappat abohakne ulhiha abohanakfish ulhiha Miko Chito micha i nan ulhtuka ulhiha, ulhtih Chuch mich Chuch chito ulhiha aiena hokono miha keyou kashke, nan ulhpisa ilappat lhupulle makinle hosh hollittop at ittoyolashke.

Aiokpache Mofimba 6, 1888.

B. F. SMALLWOOD,
Chahta Okla I Miko Chito.

BILL XXVII.

Nan anole ulhiha isht imulhtoba ai imma nan ulhpesa.

Chohta Okla nan apesa ittanahut cheya ka yakehmet ulhpisashke yohme kut Atoba 26th 1883, nan ulhpisa toba kut nan anole ulhiha isht im ulhtoba micha Kowi ulhpesa isht imulhtoba kut Kaunti iskuli isha he imissa ya ibafokket imissa kot nan ulhpisa kobaffi hochito nishan aiittimsannale ho micha nan ulhpesa chinipowa kobaffe nishan ai itti-sannale putta nan anole yosh ulhtih kot ont ahatta kut nittak achaffa aiokale ka Tule holesso achaffat iya ho Kot yamma I Choch, ak osh holisso ima ho micha kut yamma i holissoche hohchifo micha i seal aina kot alapale ho nishan i taleholesso shole ako ai im ulhtobashke; "yohme hakinle kia" hattak ut ilapo bika nun ittim akoniohme tuko Kot ut ahika ikbi putta hokuno Okla i Tuleholesso shole ya ik ik im aiulhtoba kashke. Ont achakaya ka yakohmashke, nan ulhtuka ulhiha nan anoli im annowa ulhiha keyunkmat kunuh hohkia kot yamma aya he im ulhpiesa hosh ont antta keyonkmat im annowa kiyou hosh ont antta he yoba tuk osh atta cha anumpa kʋniohmc ka̱ nan anole hokʋto isht imʋlhtoba immissa paknaka takkale yamma ikahalayokashke Nofimba 7, 1887 nan ʋlhpisa toba tokʋt moshole na nan ʋlhpisa ilappak osh alhupulle makinle hosh holittopat ittoyolashke.

Aiokpache Nofimba 6, 1888.

B. F. SMALLWOOD,
Chahta Okla I̱ Miko Chito.

BILL XXVIII.

Himakma ʋlla hollisso pisa tuchina kʋt na-huli̱-yakni hollisso apesa ia he im-issa nan ʋlhpisa.

Chahta okla nan apesa itanahʋt Chieyaka̱ yakohmit ʋlhpisʋshke. Yokmi kʋt cheki ka̱ chahta i̱ nanʋlhpisa apoksiachit itahobi tok Pech 61 micha kashkoa 6, ʋlla holisso pisa na-hulli̱-yakni ia he ai-imma yʋmmak atuk ʋt kashofa-na, ilʋppak osh ʋlhtubot fokashke—okla i̱ holisso apisa hiohli i̱ noshkoboka yak osh, ʋlla naʋkni auah-tahlapi micha ʋlla tek auah-tuklo aiena kʋt na-hulli̱-yakni holisso apisa ia chi̱ ka̱ atokola he yʋt imai-ʋlhpisashke, yohmi kʋt hannaliaiyukali hosh Chahta yakni, uhlti mia kanohmi ilʋppak atukma ai-itakash-koshke.

Nan-ʋlhpisa ilʋppʋt hlopulli makinli hosh holitopʋt itoyulashke.

Ayukpʋchi Nofimba 1, 1888.

B. F. SMALLWOOD, P. C. C. N.

BILL XXIX.

Pamit ai-imma nan ʋlhpisa.

Chata okla nan apesa itanahʋt chieyaka̱ yakahmit ʋlhpisʋshke. Hatak kana hosh nanishko ilaiyuka micha na-nawashoha itaiyuka nana hoh kia Chahta yakni anuka̱ka ka̱ ai atʋhlit a̱hanta chi̱ hakʋto Pamit ikesho kashke, yohmik ma, okla aiochuff keyu kʋt oklo ai-achʋffa keyou mak-inli ka̱ Pamit ik-imatahlo.kashke: Nan-ʋlhpisa yʋt moma keyukmat akasha̱pa kaniohmi hosh nan ʋlhpise ilʋppa̱ auet ai-i̱sanali kʋt takali hokmat moma kashofa-na, nan-ulhpisa iluppak osh hlopulli makinli hosh holitoput itoyulashke.

Ayukpochi November 6, 1888.

B. F. SMALLWOOD, P. C. C. N.

BILL XXX-

Nitak hullo nitak a wak hoyo, hliohli keyukmat itahobi ikaieno ka he nan-ulhpisa.

Chahta okla nan-aposa itanahut chieya ka yakohmit ulhpisushke. Yohmi kut nitak hullo ikowato-ka he ai-imma nan-ulhpisa Pech 170 Sakshan 36, cheki ka okla i nan-ulhpisa apoksiachit itahobi tok halafa atukla takali ka; himak a anumpa yakohmi ho ibafokit akulli, "keyukmat wak hoyo, hliohli, micha itahobi aiena ka, yohmi he ut im ai-ulhpiesa keyukuashke :"

Yohmi ak-inli kia nan-ulhpisa iluppat ulhpoa ya itahobit im-ulhtaha yosh pehlinchit apesanchi tuk o nitak hullo ut ula hokaano miha keyu kashke. Nan-ulhpisa iluppot hlopulli makinli hosh holitoput itoyulaske.

Ayukpuchi Nofimba 2, 1888.

B. F. SMALLWOOD, P. C. C. N.

BILL XXXI.

Tuli tobaksi wekichi ai-imma i nan ulhpisa Nofimba 1st, 1882, toba tok, akulli nan u lhpisa.

Chahta okla i nan-apesa itanahut chieya ka yakohmit ulhpisushke, Yohmi kut Chahta i nan-ulhpisa chiki ka apoksiachit itahobi tok, holisso putta, 89, micha kashkoa 1st, Tuli-tobaksi wekichi ai-imma i nan-ulhpisa hlafa ont 3rd anumpa "ahiohli" achi yummat kashafa.na, anumpa "Shaft" keyukmat "akola" achi kak osh ulhtubut takalashke, mikma hlafa ont 4th holisso putta holhtina micha kashkoa yummak ash inli ka anumpa "yumma" achi, anet achakaya ka iluppak osh ibafokushke, micha ik-kaniohmi nana kia awekichi ahiohli ai-asha he ai-ulhpiesa tuk ut onna-hinli hashi kanulli 7 Hiket opyaka hashi kanulli 5 ka ont aiahli; yummak keyukmat Kampeni i wekichi ulcha hut toksahanli ai-ahli ka ant ai-ahlichashke. Chahta okla nan isht im-ʊtta Agent ʊt nan-ʊlhpisa ilappa ikahlicho putta ka Miko Chito im anowacha he ʊt im ai-ʊlhpiesashke.

Nan-ʊlhpesa ilʊppʊt hlopulli mak inli hosh holitopot itoyulashke.

Ayukpʊchi Aktoba 26, 1888.

B. F. SMALLWOOD,
P. C. C. N.

BILL XXXII.

Ʊlhpoa ai-impa ya im-ʊlhtuba chi hosh kana ik-impota-ka he nan-ʊlhpisa.

SECTION 1. Chahta okla nan-apesa itanahʊt chieaka yakohmit ʊlhpisʊshke, Hatak kana hoh kia im-ʊlhtuba chi hosh kanah inla yʊt wak keyukmat nan ʊlhpoa inla nana hoh kia ai-impacha chi ka, ʊlhpoa ai-impa ya impota he ʊt im-ai-ʊlhpiesa keyu kashke.

SEC. 2. Hatak kana hosh nan-ʊlhpisa ilappa kobʊffit abanta tuk osh ʊlhtukoa hokmat Tʊli holisso Tahlepa tuklo Pokoli Tahlapi $250 ka ola keyukmat, Tahlepa Tahlapi $500 misha keyu ho aheka onotolashke. Yohmik-na okla nan isht apesa chi ho okla i Tʊli holisso sholi ako ibbak fokashke; Kaniohmit aheka ya atubba he keyu hokma ʊlhpoa ai-impa yatuk ak osh kania-na aheka micha kot atoksali tuk aiena ka isht ʊlhtubashke. Nan ʊlhpisa ilʊppʊt hlopulli makinli hosh holitopʊt itayulashke.

Ayukpʊchi Aktoba 26, 1888.

B. F. LMALLWOOD,
P. C. C. N.

BILL XXXIII.

Nan-apesa aboha toklo anumpa tosholi im-issa nan ʊlhpisa.

Chahta okla i nan-apesa itanahʊt chieya ka, yakohmit ʊlhpisʊshhe, Abo-hakni micha nakfish itatuklo kʊt okhisa-toni micha nan-ʊlhtuka ilaiyuka atokoli chatuk mako ai-itilanechi hosh, aboha toklo kʊt atokoli hosh anumpa tosholi yʊt im-asha bikashke; yumma ulhtuka ka aboha yumma pehlichi asha kak osh anumpa kullo yá onochashke. Nitak aiyukali isht im-ulhtuba yut aboha yumma ai-achuffa isht im-ulhtuba yak-inli ho ai-itilauashke; aboha ya itanahut chieya aiyukali ka anumpa tosholi uhleha ahanchi kash yummat, ai-ibatakla chieya-na biliyashke, micha nan-apesa ai-achuffa kanima kut ahnikma anumpa ha toshohonlashke. Nan-ulhpisa iluppat ahlopulli mak-inli hosh holittoput itoyulashke.

Ayukpuchi Aktoba 26, 1898.

B. F. SMALLWOOD,
P. C. C. N.

BILL XXXIV.

Chahta Okla I Talcholesso shole ya atonachi Nan ulhpisah hut toba tok a nan ulhpisa hut akulle.

Chahta Okla nan apisa ittanaha chito ittafamat cheya ka yakohmet ulhpisashke, Nofimba 9, 1887, a nan ulhpisa toba cha holitopa tok sekshan atukla ka afoyokka kat Chahta Okla I tule holesso shole ya atona chi apisa tok yammut yakohmit ulhkatashke. Issuba ombinile tuklo yammat Taleholesso shole ako ai I nataka hosh heyelashke, mikmat tikba kash issuba ombinili chakkale hosh ulhtukat hile taka ibafokkashke mikma yakohmashke, achi ilappat ulhpisat alhupulle ka alhet holettopat ittoyolashke.

Aiokpachi October 16, 1888.

B. F. SMALLWOOD,
Chahta Okla I Miko Chito.

BILL XXXV.

Tale tobakse ai imma nan ittimapesa ya Nofimba 6, 1880, a nan ulhpisa toba tok a nan ulhpisa hut akalle.

Chahta Okla nan apisa ittannaha chito ittafamat cheya ka yakohmet ulhpisashke. Chahta Okla I nan-ulhpisa holisso toba tok (page 85), micha lhafa isht ontuchchina ka micha anumpa tobakse kulle achi pammak fihna annumpa yakohme hosh ibafokkashke (micha tale akulle) mikma nan ulhpisa hot alhkatakmat ittim annumpa kot yakohmashke Nan ittim apisa (contract) at nan ulhpisa ilappak-atukma ai I nutakat toba poyottak kut Tesemba 31. Aioka ho ont ai ulhlhashke, yohmikma Tabakse micha Tale kulle aina hokoto afamme hannalli ho ont ai ulhlhashke yohmikma ilappak atukma ai I nutaka putta ka neshan isht im ulhtoba (Royalty) at hashe achuffa aioka ka ulhtoba he ai ulhpeyesashke.

Mikma nan ulhpisa ilappat alhupulle ka ai alhet iya ka ai alhet holittopat ittoyolashke.

Aiokpache October 15, 1888.

B. F. SMALLWOOD,
Chahta Okla I Miko Chito.

BILL XXXVI.

Atoka Kaunte ai Anukaka nan atohole nan isht ayasha ya chi ka nan ulhpisa hut hilechit imissa.

Chahta Okla nan apesa ittanaha chito ittafumat Cheya ka yakohmit ulhpesashke. Atoka County, ai anukaka micha Atoka Tamaha ya I falamme pila imma koweh pokole ushta fokka micha Austin Wever. I chukka ya Im Oka-mahle imma koweh achuffa fokka ho nan atokole nan isht ayasha ut hikkeyashke micha Nosape nanih nan atokole nan isht ayasha hoh chifashke.

Mikma nan ulhpesa ilappat Alhupulle Ka ayahlt iya kat ai alhet holettopat ittoyutashke.

Aiokpuche October 22nd, 1888.

B. F. SMALLWOOD,
Chahta Okla I miko Chito.

BILL XXXVII.

Atoka County anukaka nan atokole nanisht ayasha ya nan ulhpesa hut helechit.

Chahta Okla nan apesa ittanaha Chito ittafumat Cheya ka yakohmet ulhpesashke. Atoka County Chahta yakne, ai annkaka ya nan atokule nan isht aiy asha at Atoka Tamaha I f alamme hashe akuchcha ai ittintakla imma kowe pukole tuklo

akuch cha untukle fokka micha George Lawys ai atta ya I hopaka kut ulhpesa talhepa Achuffa fukka ho Lhabeta Isketine holisso apisa chukka at hikeya yammako ahikkeya cha Lhabita Isketine nan atokole nan isht ayusha hohohifoshke.

Mikma nan ulhpesa illappat lhupulla ka ai ulhet iya kat ai alhet holettopat ittoyolashke.

Ai Okpache Oetober 26, 1888.

B. F. SMALLWOOD,
Chahta Okla I Miko Chito.

XXXVIII.

Imomukpuli ikhopokoyo micha imanukfilikono aina isht apilache nan ulhpisa hut imissa.

Chahta okla nan apisa ittanaha chito ittafamat chieya ka yakohmit ulhpisashke. Yohme kut Chahta okla ai achuffa kanah hosh imomukpulo yatuk osh konioht ilapilacha he keyou micha isht ilapelache ut ik imuksho mikma ikhopokoyo micha imanukfilikono aina ka Tule holesso Pokole tulhape aioka ho Okla i tule holisso shole ako ai im ulhtobashke, Yohmikma ilap i Kaunti Chuch ulhiha aioka kak osh ai ulhpiesa ahnit aiopachit Satifikit o ima hokmakashke, micha yammak osh nan ulhpisa ilappa ai iyakkaya ho isht ilapilache iskule isha chi tuk a apisanchit yakohme ahna he ut im ai ulhpiesashke. Yohmikma nan ulhpesa ilappa moma hokma keyoukmat akashampa hokma nana hokia asanule kut tikba alhupulle tok ut akshot mosholashke. Yohmikma nan ulhpisa ilapput alhupulle ka ai ulhit iya ka aiyalhit holittopat ittoyolashke.

Aiokpache Nofimba 7, 1888.

B. F. SMALLWOOD,
Chahta Okla I Miko Chito.

BILL XXXIX.

Milishi Nan ulhpisa ha nan ulhpisa hut yikoble.

Chahta okla nan apisa ittanaha chito ittafamat cheya ka yakohmit ulhpesashke, Yohmi kut Nofimba 3, 1883, a Chahta

okla hct milishi ct clhtokat I heyola he nan ulhpisa ut alhupullet hoitopa tok a yammak atuk ut Yekopashke. Yakomashke Aehe iiappat alhuplle ka ai ulhit iya kat holittopat ittoyulayshke.

Aiokpache Nofimba 7, 1888.

B. F. SMALLWOOD,
Chahta Okla I Miko Chito.

BILL XL.

Kamishi kaunte. C. N., anukaka ya kulih kashofa kot yakne ya nan clhpisa hct kanclleche.

SECTION 1. Chahta Okla nan apisa ittancha chito ittafamat cheya ka yakohmit clhpisashke Kamishi kaunti ai anukaka ya kclih koshofa kot yakne yat Kanallit kaunti achi kash anukaka ya St. Louis micha Sanfrancisco, tale hina abaiya Goodland Station ako ont hikkiya cha Goodland kot yakne hohchifashke.

SEC. 2. Ont achakaya ka yakohmit clhpisashke, Goodland kot yakne achi kash kot ai ittafoma cmmona kct Chanoele mate cmmona 1890, micha yomma ai clhit misha mahaya ka hcshi inla aioka mate cmmona ka ai ittafahamashke.

SEC. 3. Ont achakaya ka yakohmit ulhpesashke Kaunte achi kash ycmma i chcch akosh yohma he ct im ai clhpiesa cha hattak nan isht ctta imponna tuklo keyoukmat atampa kia atokule na ycmmakosh, tekba ka kot chukka atuk kclih kcshofa yomma kot chukka ya nittak pokole tuchchina moma ho isht annowa holisso ha hattak aittonaha chatuk mia tuchchina ka kaunte achi kash anoka ka lapulechi cha kanchashke, mikma isht clhtoba yct kot chukka himona ako isht ulhtahcshke.

SEC. 4. Ont achakaya ka yakohmit ulhpisashke nan clhpisa ilappat alhupulle makinle hosh holittoput ittoyolashke.

Aiokpachi October 28, 1889.

B. F. SMALLWOOD,
Chata Okla i Miko Chito.

BILL XLI.

Kiamichi County ai anukaka nan atokole nah isht ayasha ya nan ulhpisa hut Kunulleche.

SECTION 1. Chahta Okla nan opisa ittanaha chito ittafamat cheya ka yakohmet ulhpisushke yohme kut Kiamichi County aiannkaka ya nan atokole nan isht aiyash, tekba ka kulih kash-ufa hohchifo chatuk yammat kunulle St. Louis mich San Francisco tulebina abaiya Goodland Station ako ont hik-keya cha, Goodland, nan atokole nan isht aiyasha hohchifashke.

SEC. 2. Ont achaka yakohmet ulhpisashke nan atokle nan isht ayasha Goodland ache kash, ai ittafuma ummona kut August winste ummona 1890. Yako micha yumma ai ulhit misha mahaya ka yumma ko yummak ai ittafahamashke.

Mikma nun ulhpisa ilappat alhupulle mak inle hosh holltlopat ittoyolashke.

Aiokppoche Oktoba 28, 1889.

B. F. SMALLWOOD,
Chahta Okla i Miko chito.

BILL XLII.

Chahta Okla ai achoffa toba bunna yut akoniohma he nan ulhpisa hut im imapisa.

Chahta Okla nan apisa ittanaha chito ittafamat cheya ka yakohmit ulhpisashke. Himak pila mahaya ka Chahta Okla ai achuffa toba bunna ulhiha hut okla ai achuffa toba bunnat asilhha. Aioka kut Chahta Okla i Taliholesso shole ya Toleholesso tulhepa achuffa $100 ho im atobbashke. Yohmikma yakohmashke achi paknaka takkale kako ai iyakkaya ho okla i tuli holesso shole ut holisso (receipt) ima ho okla ai achuffa toba buna annumpa ashlha ya ittainichi hosh bohle ho keyou hokuno, nan isht asha Komitte ut isht im asho kashke, mikma nan ulhpisa ilappat alhupulle hai a ai-ulhit mahaya ka holettopat ittoyolamak oke.

Aiokpachi November 6, 1888.

B. F. SMALLWOOD,
Chahta Okla I Miko Chito.

BILL XLIII.

Holisso apisa hochito holisso pisa ʋt ak-ʋniahma he ai imma nan ʋlhpisa ya̱ nan ʋlbpisa hʋt akʋlle.

Chahta okla nan apisa ittanaha chito ittafʋmat cheya̱ ka̱ yakohmit ʋlhpesʋshke, Nofimba 1842, nan ʋlhpisa toba tok a̱ chi̱ke ka̱ Chahta okla i̱ nan ʋlhpisa holisso toba tok a̱ Page (67) paknaka ya̱ Chapta ʋmmana micha Sekshan 5 mikmat kashkowa 4 aioyokka kʋt ittim annumpa kʋt yakomishke.

Chata i̱ yakne ilappa̱ holesso apisa hochito poyutta ka̱ chukka chʋffa naha hohkia holisso pisa achʋffa ka̱ misha keyou ho̱ bohlashke ache yʋmmat yakohmit ʋlhkatʋshke. Chahta yakne ilappa̱ holesso apisa hochito heyohle kakokma keyoukmat nahullo i̱ yakne, (Istets,) akokma nana hoh kia Chahta okla im iskʋle yosh isht ʋlhtoba ho̱ holisso pisa chi̱ poyutta ka̱ Chukka chʋffa nana hoh kia holisso pisa ʋt achʋffa ka̱ misha. keyou ho̱ bohlashke.

Sek. 2. Chahta yakne ilappa̱ holisso apisa hochito heyohle kak okma keyoukmat nahullo i̱ yakne (Istets) ak okma nana hohkia chukka choffa nana hosh holisso pisa achʋffa ka̱ misha yo̱ bohle tuk ma holisso apisa yʋmma i̱ nushkoboka (Supotentan) ʋt isht ʋlhtoka holisso Satifikit atukma i̱ moshole chi cha achuffa kak bʋno ho̱ i̱ holitoblechashke, mikmat mihmakinle ho̱ yʋmma isht alota chi̱ ka̱ isht awakayashke. Mikma nan ʋlhpisa ilappʋt alhupulli ka̱ Akʋs ʋmmona 1890, misha maha̱ya ai alhit holittopʋt ittoyolashke.

Aiokpachi Tisimba 20, 1889.

B. F. SMALLWOOD,
Mi̱ko Chito.

BILL XLIV.

Kamishi Kaunti ai anuka̱ka nan ai atokole ya̱ nan ʋlhpisa hʋt konʋlleche.

Chahta okla nan apisa ittanaha chito ittafamat cheyu ka̱ yakohmit ʋhlpisashke, Kamishi kaunti ai-nukaka ya̱ nan atokole nan isht ai asha, Lakstʋn ʋt Kʋnʋllet Lakstan achi kash im oka mahle kowe iklʋnno ho̱ iti abasha ai ittanʋha yʋmmako̱ pit ahikkia cha iti abusha nan ai atokole hochifashke. Mikma nan ulhpisa illappat alhupulle hai yut ai alhet kullot ittoyulashke.

Aiokpachi Nofimba 20, 1889.

B. F. SMALLWOOD,
Miko Chito.

BILL XLV.

Chata yakne ilappa tule ilaioka akula kuniohmit a mahaya chi ka nan ulhpisa hut im issa.

Yakohmishke, Chahta okla hut nan ithana mikmat nana ilaioka isht ulhtaha he a Tuli holisso ut ibalhkuhat i shaht mahaya he ut ai ulhpiesashke.

Yohme hatuko; Yakomishke, Tuli ilauka hokut ik ottuno kisha hosh yakni anukaka yatukma ai ahsashke. Yohme kia ahaiochi cha kulli keyou hokuno, isht ai oncholowa, himonese ai asha keyoukmat himak pila mehinte kak oh kia nan isht im ai chukma chi kut ikshoshke, Yohme hatuko.

SEK. 1. Chahta okla nan apesa ittanuha chito ittafmut chey ka yakohmit ulhpisashke. Chahta okla ai achuffa kuna hosh Tuli kullo keyokmat nake keyoukmat Tulitobaksi okma nana ho ahayuchi hokmut yumma i kowi achuffa folota ka atoksala he ut im ai ulhpisashke. Yohmi hakinle kia kaunti kunimma ho Tuli akola nana ho ahayochi hatukmut yumma i kaunti i holissuche ako tikba holisso afukki hai ashke. Ont achakaya ka yakohmi hokmak ashke. Tuli kuniohme hatukma akanchi ya akunia chi moma ka alhtuha hokma yumma ittiyulle ai ulhpiesa ka (pasint 6) ka Chahta, micha Chikashah, ai ina ka im atobbashke yohmikma Chahta yut (pasint 6) achi kash, kashkowa tuchina kako (3-4) ako ishashke mikma Chikasha hut kashkowa aioshta (1-4) ako ishashke, Yohmi kia yak-ohme hokmak-ashke, Chahta okla nan isht im utta-(Echun) ako tikba nan ittim apisa ittimikbi kut nan amia micha akuniohme putta kut Tuli tobaksi kulle ya ittim atahle chatuk ako ittilawi hashke.

Aiokpache.

B. F. SMALLWOOD,
Miko Chito.

BILL XLVI.

Okla ai-achuffa tuba bunna nan ulhpisa Aktoba 21, 1882, toba tok mosholichi nan-ulhpisa.

Okla i nan-apesa ma, Chi Kummiti piaha, Miko chito ut Aktoba 21, 1882 Chahta okla nan isht imai-ulhpiesa ya aiachota ilemihut nan-asilhha bohli-na, "nana-apesa tuk kia," achakala he im-issa yut moshola he ahnit anumpa pi boho li tuk a achukmalit anukfillit epihinsa mat, nan.ulhpisa anet iyakaya iluppak osh hlopulli hokbano ahnit echi-bohli ka iluppak oke:

SECTION 1. Chahta okla i nan-apesa itanahut chieyaka, yakohmit ulhpisashke, Hatak kana hosh okla nan-isht im-aiulhpisa ya aiachuffa ilemihut nan-asilhha bohli-na, okla i nan-apesa ak osh kanimihchit apesa hokma, yummak osh ont ai-ahlashke, yohmikma, Aktoba 21, 1882 nan-ulhpisa tuba tok ut moynmyt mosholashke. Nan-ulhpisa iluppat hlopulli mak-inle hosh holitoput itoynlashke.

Ai-okpuchi Aktoba 30, 1889.

BILL XLVII.

Kummishuna tuchina hosh ulhtuka cha U. S. Kummishuna uhleha ulhti pota ai-imma micha nana inla ai-ilaiyukali ka nan-isht itimapesa he nan-ulhpisa.

Yakohmishke, Mey 28, 1830, kunkilus nan-ulhpisa i hikbi tok mako aiiyakaya hosh Yunatit Stets i Miko ut himonasi hatak upi-homa i yakni ilappa yakmikchit in-talali ka micha oklushi uhleha ha "aiahli mak osh imili-kahanli" kut, yumma im-ulla uhleha, keyukmat isht ai-onchololi uhleha hut aiahashwa micha immih abilia chi hatok;

Atuko yakohmiske, Kunkilus nan-ulhpisa ihikbi tok mako ai-iyakaya hosh Yunatit Stets i Miko ut ont Septimba ma, Chahta okla ha Cholite itim-ihikbi kut, himonasi aiahashwa micha tikba ka im-issa tok a aienichi hosh im-issa tok;

Atuko yakohmishke, 1855, Choliti tohomba tok atikul 9 yumma Chahta Okla micha Chikasha okla aiena kut Talitoli ai-itibahalulli chatuk yakni ulhpisa 98 i hashi ai-opyaka imma yumma kashapa ho "Kufamant" ut Wishita micha oklushi uhleha keyukmat hatak upi-homa nana hoh kia ilaiasha-chashke, ahni hokmut yamih cha chi ho im pota tok ;

Yohmi ak-inli kia Chahta okla micha Chikasha okla aien kʋt, yʋmma ont aiahanta bonna hokmʋt im ai-ʋlpiesa chi ka imissa tok ;

Atuko yakohmishke, Siptimba 9, 1865, ash Holitopa D. N. Cooley hatak ʋpi-homa nan-isht im ʋtta, Holitopa Elijah Sells oka-mahli i Supt. Thomas Wister ikana ʋhleha ai itapeha, Yunatit Stets in-toshka chipota i nan-ʋlhtuka W. S. Harney, Chanʋl Grant i nan-ʋlhtuka Kanʋl Ely S. Parker aiena ka Yunatit Stets i Miko ʋt Bot Kʋmmishʋna achi hosh atokoli cha nan-isht ai ahlika micha yʋmmak ash Yunatit Stets i Miko ʋlhtuba mak osh, Chahta okla i Kʋmmishʋna ʋhleha ha ont imotaninchi ka Choliti ʋt nanah inla ai-ilaiyuka yakohmi kʋt ai-ibafokit itibachʋffa ka yakohmishke.

5. Chahta okla micha Chikasha okla aiena kʋt i yakni ash ai ahashwa tuk, yʋmma akashapa ka oklushi nan aiya Kansas micha inlaka ai ahashwa tuka ako in-talalishke ; ont achakaya ka yakmih-chit itibachʋffashke.

7. Nahullo nan-ʋlhtuka, Echant, micha okla talaya i tisho, keyukmʋt yakni ilʋppak-inli anukaka nan-atahla chi ho kʋfamant ʋt im-issa tok, keyukmʋt oklushi i nan-ʋlhpisa mako aiyakaya hosh iba-holhtina tok ʋhleha, yʋmmak illa hosh Talitoli anukaka ka ai-ahashwa he ʋt imai-ʋlhpiesashke ;

Atuko yakohmishke, Yunatit Stets Kʋmmishʋna achi kash ant haiyakama yakni hashi ai opyaka yakni ʋlhpisa 98 talaya Chahta micha Chikasha aiena kʋt abinila he imai-ʋlhpiesa kash, hatak ʋpi-homa nan-aiya micha Chahta, Chikasha okla aiena i yuka-issa ʋhleha aiena kʋt, mominchit nan-anukfilli micha abinila he ʋlhpisa, yʋmmat Chahta, micha Chikasha okla aiena kʋt il a-hotihnʋchit ishi keyu hokma, micha Chahta, Chikasha aiena kʋt 1866, Choliti itim-ikbi tok atekʋl 3rd ka yakni ʋlhpisa 98 i hashi ai-opyaka yakni talaya ka Yunatit Stets i kʋnchi kʋt chashpo ka nana ho akani-micha he aknli tok ʋt, yʋmmak achi ho halʋlli, yohmi cha Yunatet Stets i nan-ʋlhpisa micha Choliti itim-ihikbi tok ahanchi kash yʋmmak o ai-inutaka he atok ;

Atuko yakohmishke, March 1, 1889, Kʋnkilʋs ʋt nanʋlhpisa ikbi ho Muskoki micha Simanoli i yakni aiena kʋt Chahta okla hʋt i yakni hashi ai-opyaka pila holhtina 98 talayaka ikʋnchi kʋt nana ho akaniohma he atok a yʋmmak-inli ho ai itilawa he atok akinli kia, chumpa putta hosh, hatak ʋpi-homa ʋt abinila he atoka kobahaffishke ;

Atuko yakohmishke, Yunatit Stets ʋt Kʋnkilʋs March 2, 1889, nan-ʋlhpisa ihikbi ho, nanah himona mih-mak o Yunatit Stets i Miko ʋt aiiyakaya hosh, Kʋmmishʋna tuchina ka atokoli kʋt, hatak ʋpi homa poyutta kʋt i yakni anukaka holhtina 96 ka i hashi ai-opyaka pila ahalʋlli putta, micha nan-isht imai-ʋlhpiesa ai-ilaiyukali putta tuka, nana ka isht itim-apesa chi ho atokoli tuk ;

Atuko yakohmishke, Yunatit Stets ʋt nana ka ai-inlacha he ahni ka, micha hatak ʋpi-homa i yakni hashi ai-opyaka pila ha Kʋfamant ʋt Talitoli i nan-ʋlhpisa abohli bʋnna, micha hashi ai-opyaka pila holhtina 98 ka hatak ʋpi-homa nan-aiya ʋhlcha ak osh ai asha chi ho 1866 ash im-issa tok ak-inli kia, nanah inla ho akani-micha he ahni ka, yakohmi ai-ahnishke ;

Mihma yakohmishke, Yunatit Stets nan-ai ahni kʋt, Chahta okla micha ilap ai-achʋffa ʋhleha ai-imma ho nana ka isht anuk-filli hokma, ibai-ʋkpanchi micha yohmi hokbano ai-ahni chatuk, yohmi hoka, yakohmashke.

Sakshʋn 1. Chata okla i nan-apesa itanahʋt chieyaka, yak-ohmit ʋlhpisashke. Chahta okla i Miko chito ʋt ayohma he ʋt imai-ʋlhpiesa cha, abo-hakni hʋt ibai-okpʋnchi ho hatak oka-homi ishko keyu tuchina ho Kʋmmishʋna atokoli-na Chahta okla ha akucha hosh hashi ai-opyaka pila yakni holhtina 98 micha 100 ai-itintakla imma micha Bok-homa, Canadian Bok itintakla yakni eka 7,713,239 ilappa isht itafamashke.

Sak. 2. Kʋmmishʋna ʋhleha achi kash, Kʋnkilʋs ʋt March 2, 1889, nan-ʋlhpisa ikbi tok mak o ai-iyakaya hosh kʋmmishʋna ʋlhtukʋt aya, keyukmat Chahta okla i yakni hashi ai-opyaka pilʋ holhtina 98 talaya nan-isht imai-ʋlhpiesa ai-ilaiyukali putta ka Yunatit Stets i kʋncha he ahni ka nan-isht itim-apesashke : kʋmmishʋna ʋhleha achi kash, yakni ilappa Okla-homa Talitoli ya hi ahni kʋt ai-iba-foka he ahni hokma, yichienʋt, amosholi hosh asa-nahanli-na, Chahta okla immih ha he ai-ʋlhpiesa tuk a im-issa hayashke.

Sak. 3. Kʋmmishʋna ʋhleha achi kash, nan-ʋlhpisa ilappʋt nan ai ahni ka Chikasha okla hʋt ai-iba-chʋffʋt, ita-kʋlla he a im-ahnashke ; yohmi cha Yunatit Stets i nan-ʋlhtuka ʋhleha ha kani-mihchi hosh nana ka itim-apesa hokmut, chikosi nan-anoa ha Miko chito i bohlashke, yohmi kia, kummishuna achi kash nan-itim-apesa fuka, okla i nan-apesapakosh imai-okpunchi keyu hokano ik-holitopo-kashke ; Miko chito ut ayohma he ut imai-ulhpiesa cha kummishuna ut kani-mihchit nana ka itim-apesa cha im-annoachi makinli ho okla i nan-apesa a itafamichashke.

SAK. 4. Kummishuna uhleha achi kash, okla nan-isht im ahanta takla kut isht im ulhtuka yut nitak achuffakma Tuli holisso hannali micha kowi achuffak-ma sint pokolitiashke ; ilap inli hosh satifikit ikbi ho Miko ut im ai-okpunchi ho im ulhtubashke, micha nanah kania ka isht ulhtuba ulhpesa aiena kut nan-isht ulhpisa keyu Toli-holisso sholi ibbak fuka kut isht ulhtuba chi hosh ulhpisashke ; ont achakayaka, yakohmit ulhpisashke.

Nan-ulhpisa iluppat ahlopulli makinli hosh holitoput itoyalashke.

Ai-okpuchi November 5, 1889.

BILL XLVIII.

Chahta okla i nan apesa aboha tuklo yakohmashke achi:

Yakohmishke, nan ai ulthtukoa anoliha hinli hosh, okla iluppa im-unnoahanchi, yohmikma St. Louis micha San Francisco. Tuli-hina i nan-ulhtuka uhleha hut yohma he ahni-na, holisso kia afokut okla ha im-ottahunni kut, Kumpeni achi kash, yummat, himak pila Yunatit Stets nan-upesu ut itafamak-ma Californila micha St- Louis Tuli-hina hoh-chihifo ho hatak upihoma i yakni a aolopullicha chi ka Kunkilus ut imissa he ahnit, nan-asilhha i bohla chi kut anumpa atahli hosh aiash, yohmi kut St. Louis micha San Francisco Kumpeni achi kash osh immih micha yummak osh nan-amikfihinli :

Mikma, yakohmishke, Tuli-hina ataya he asilhha ka moma kut kowi 2000 ka ont ia, micha yakni Tuli-hina atomba hinla ka mominchi ; yohmi cha Tuli-hina ikbi kut Kunkilus im-issa toko Tuli-hina ulhtaha bachayaka ai-itapotulichi micha hatak upi-homa i yakni anukaka ka Tuli-hina tuba he ai-imma ka ila-mominchi cha, tikba he ai-imma ka ila-mominchi che, tikba ka St. Louis micha San Francisco Tuli-hina hoh-chihifo beka tou ut, California micha St. Louis micha San Francisco ako im-issa, yohmi cha inla ka putta ka im-okshihta, yohmi-na hatak ʋpi-homa i yakni ahanchi kash ai-achʋffa yʋt nana ka ,sht impalʋmmi :

Yohmi ka yakohmishke. Yunatit Stets ʋt hatak ʋpi-homa oklushi mia tahlapi ka afʋmmi 1866, anukaka Cholite itim ikbit im-issa kʋt, Tʋli-hina achʋffa hosh Falʋmmi micha oka-mahli aieya hatak ʋpi-homa i yakni achi achi kash ahlopullit Tʋli-hina yʋt bachaya he atok; yohmikma hashi akucha micha ai-opyaka aiena ka Taletoli achi kash ahlopullit bachaya he atok; Atoko yakohmishke, Falʋmmi micha okamahli aiena ka Tʋli-hina a-hi atok a Missouri, Kansas micha Texas Tʋli-hina aiena kak osh Tʋli-hina ai-atahli tok, mihma hashi akuchaka micha ai opyaka Tʋli-hina abachaya he atok a, Chahta Tʋli-tobaksi micha Tʋli-hina i kʋmcpeni ak osh eshi tok osh himonase ka Tʋli-hina ai-atahli hosh ashwahanchishke.

Yohmi-ma, yakohmishke ; 1866 Cholite itim ikbit Tʋli-hina ataya he im-issa tok a ont atʋmpa ka. Yuuatit Stets kʋnkilʋs ʋt Tʋli-hina inlaka nitak ai-ilaiyukali ka, hatak ʋpi-homa i yakni achi kash ahlopulla chi ho immi-hinsa tʋkokaniohmi kʋt tobʋt ʋlhtaha, yohmikma inla ʋt isht awakaya ; yohmi hatuko yakohmishke ; okla tʋlaya kʋt Taletoli ilʋppa nan-akaniohmi putta kʋt okla lokoli achʋffa ho ai-imominchi, micha inla putta kano imokshihta, yohmi cha Yunatit States ʋt 1866, Chohtite nan ai-itemi hinsa tok, micha Taletoli a im-ili-kahahli tok ʋt, Tʋli-hina inlaka imi-hisisa putta kʋsh koba-haffishke ;

Yohmi hatuktlo, yakohmashke, Chahta okla i nan-apesa ab-oha tuklo itafamat chieyaka yakohmashke, St. Louis micha San Francisco Tʋli-hina hoh-chihifo beka tok ʋt. California micha St. Louis Tʋli-hina achi kash, Tʋli-hina ataya he' asilhaa tuka "aiahli mak osh ilai-isannali," micha yʋmmak okʋt, hatak ʋpi-homa ai-achʋffa nan-isht im ai-ʋchokma nan-isht isht im ai-ʋlhpissa ya ai-okpanichi micha yʋmma itimpakna chi hosh isht awakaya tuk a Cholite nan-ai-immi-hinsa tok a ont atompli hokano moshola he ako apissali ; yohmi hatuk o, Yunatit Stets kʋnkilʋs a inutakʋt ilim-otaninchi kʋt St. Louis micha San Francisco Tʋli-hina, yʋmmat California micha St. Louis Tʋli-hina hoh-chihifo, Tʋli-hina ataya he asilhha ya im-issa ho mʋhli hokma, kʋmpeni inla kʋt Talitole annkaka ka Tʋli-hina ai-ikba he tuk kia imoktvbli, micha nitak inla mihinti ka ai-itapeba achvffa ho Tvli- hina ai-imma putta ka, oklushi mia tahlapi, aiachvffa vbleha hvt ai-inutaka hos hiela he :

Ont achakayaka, yakomishke nitak olbvlaka St. Louis micha San Erancisco Talitole anukaka nana akaniohmi tuk a cpheinsa,yohmi ka Tvli-hina ahanchi kash hina ataya he asilhha chi hosh anumpa atahli tuk, micha ai-itapeba achvffa yvmmat yvmma asilhha kvt ai-itapeba inla kvt Taletoli anukaka ka nana ka isht aiabashwa he ahni tuk a micha nana ka atahlit nanisht ai-itimpakna he tuk a ataklvmmichi micha nukshobli aiena he ako ahni ; Ont achakayaka, Yunatit Stets kvnvilvs a inutakvt ilahn-ahanchi kvt St. Louis micha San Francisco Tvli-hina achi kash yvmmat Talitoli ilvppa Tvli-hina ahlopullicha he a im issa toko halvlli-na himak a atvmmi pokali-tuklo akinli kia yvmma ikbi tok keyu micha ikbi hosh ashwahanche keyushke; Ontachakayaka, yakohmashke aboha tuklo yakohmashke achi ilvppa Nashinvl Sakliteli vt hobachit Yunatit Stets i Miko micha Sakiiteli Intelia, abo-hakni i Miko micha abohanakfish im anumpa eeshi Yunatit Stets Emalika chieyaka pit i bohlashke :

Ont achakayaka, yakohmashke resolution ilvppvt hlopulli mak-inlihosh holitopvt itoyulashke.

Ai-okpnchi Nofimba 5, 1889.

BILL XLIX.

Aheka sipokni itiuyupelvcha he nan-vlhpisa toba tok yikobli nan-vlhpisa.

SEKSHVN 1. Chahta okla i nan-apesa itenahvt chieaka, yakohmit vlhpiesashke. Nov. 6, 1888, "net ploset" iskali itiyupelvcha he Kvmmishan vlhtuka he nan vlhpisa tobvt holitopa tok, micha Channali 18, 1889, nan-vlhpisa tuba tok, akvlli nanvlhpisa tuba tok, itatuklo ka yikoblichishke.

SEK. 2. Ont achakayaka, yakohmit vlhpisashke, Net ploset i Kvmmishan achi kash, holisso, Lepot, Takit micha holisso nana hosh Kvmmishan nan-isht ai-asha tok yvmma ahalaya putta ka mominchit Nashinvl Sakliteli nan-isht ai-vtta ashachina, nan-apesa okla hʊt apehinsashke. Nan-ʊlhpisa ilʊp pʊt hlopulli mak-inli hosh holitopʊt itʊyulashke.

Aiokpʊchi, Aktoba 30, 1889.

BILL L.

Kʊmmiti tuchina hosh ʊlhtaka-cha U. S. Kʊmmishʊna ʊleha ʊlhti pota ai-imma micha nana inla ai-ilaiyukali nan-isht itim-apesa chi̱ "nan-isht amia" nan ʊlhpisa Nov. 5, 1889, toba tok akashạpa kạ mosholichi nan-ʊlhpisa.

Chahta okla i̱ nan-apesa itanahʊt chieyakạ, Yakohmit ʊlhpisashke, Cʊmmiti tuchina hosh ʊlhtuka cha, U. S. Kʊmmishʊna ʊhleha, ulhti pota ai-imma micha nana inla ai-ilaiyukali nan-isht itim-apesa he "nan-isht amia" nan-ʊlhpisa Nov. 5, 1889, toba tok ʊt; itim-anumpa kʊt yakohmi, "Chahta okla hʊt 1837, Choleti ikbi hosh i̱ yakni moyuma kạ akash-koa ont isht ai-ushta kạ Chikasha okla hạ i̱ kanchi tok" achi, illʊpak atuk ʊt mosholashke.

Ai-okpachi Nov. 9, 1889,

BILL LI.

Wak hobak Chahta yakni isht chukowoa he im-issa nan-ʊlhpisa, imoktʊbli nan-ʊlhpisa mosholichi nan-ʊlhpisa.

Chahta okla i̱ uan-apesa itanahʊt chieyakạ, yakohmit ʊlhpisashke, Wak hobak Chahta yakni ishtik-chukow ka he imoktubli; amba Nofimba micha Tisimba hashi anụkạka kak illa he nan-ʊlhpisa tobʊt ahlopulli tok osh Aktoba 30, 1888, fehna nitak ʊt ont intaha cha, ilʊp inlit nan-ʊlhpisa tuba tok, yʊmmʊt himak okano mosholashke.

Nan-ʊlhpisa ilʊppʊt hlopulli mak-inli hosh holitopʊt itoyulashke.

Ai-okpʊchi Nofimba 13, 1889.

BILL LII.

Wade Kaunti kot yakni kanʊllichi nan-ʊlhpisa.

Chahta okla i̱ nan-apesa itanahʊt chieyakạ, yakohmit ʊlhpi-

sashke. Kaunti kot yakni Wade Kaunti ko̱chʋt-o̱wakah kot yakni ʋt Tʋli-hina ako̱ pit kanʋllashke, yohmi cha Tʋli-hina kot yakni isht ahoh-chi̱hi̱fashke.

Wade Kaunti a̱ kaunti kot isht ai-asha ʋmmo̱na kʋt Chanuali Manti ʋmmo̱na kak ashke. Nan-ʋlhpisa ilʋppʋt hlopulli tuk a̱ Tesimba 31, 1889, okmako̱ holitopʋt itoyulat ma̱ha̱yashke.

Ai-okpʋchi Nofimba 13, 1889.

BILL LIII.

Mi̱ko chito ʋt Intilia Tepatman a̱ nan-a a kaniohmi ka̱ imahoya he im-ahni nan ʋlhpisa.

Chahta okla i̱ nan-apesa itanahʋt chieyaka̱, yakohmit ʋlhpisashke.

Robert L. Owen, U. S. Hatak ʋpi-homa nan-isht im-ʋtta a̱ Chahta i̱ yuka-issa kaniohmi aiyukali hosh Choleti 1866, Atekʋl 3rd nan amia ka̱ ai-iyakaya hosh Neshʋn akucha chi̱ hosh ʋlhtuka tok ʋt otaiyani bokma ima-tubba chi̱ ho̱ yuka issa im iskali a̱ ibbak foki tok a̱, nanah kania, micha kaniohmi aiyukali ho̱ ima-tubbi tok, micha holhtina kaniohmi, micha hoh-chifo nana aiyukali hosh im-ʋlhtuba tok, micha laua kaniohmi hosb ik imʋlhtuba tok amoyuma ka̱ ai-in-tokoa micha iskali ʋt atʋmpʋt itonla yuba-na U. S. Hatak ʋpi-homa nan-isht im-ʋtta yʋt falamichit bohli tok okma; yʋmmat akaniohmi tok aiena ka̱ Mi̱ko chito ʋt Intelia Tipatman a̱ nan-anoah ima-hoyashke.

Nan ʋlhpisa ilʋppʋt hlhpulli mak-inli hosh holitopʋt itoyulashke.

Ai-okpʋchi November 13, 1889.

BILL LIV.

Nan-ʋlhpisa osh im-issa keyu ho̱ Yunatit Stets kot ahiohli-hinchi ka̱, Chahta okla micha aiachuffa ʋlheba aiena nan isht imai-ʋlhpiesa apehpoachi̱ nan-ʋlhpisa.

Yakohmishke, 1866 Choliti tuba tok atikʋl 38, mako̱ aiiyakaya hosh nahullo yʋt Chahta okla ai achuffa nan-isht imaiʋlhpiesa ai-ilaiyukoli putta, Bot i̱ kania, nan-ʋlhtuka ishi, micha nan-ʋlhpisa kobafa putta ka̱ Chahta i̱ kot foki micha fokka, yohmi kvt Chahta ako atoba tok a ai-itilanit nan-imvlhpihinsvt isht aue-hinchi toka hopakishke:

Atuko yakahmishke, Stephen Belvin vt Chahta issish o ilaieshi osh, achvffa A. E. Powell vt iti-halvlli hosh Chahta okla ai achvffa ya tuko vbi tok osh anumpa isht ai-onotayula-na ulhti 3rd i kot Chahta yakni isht aiasha he ont ai-vlhpiesa February a ont haiyaka-na, nan-isht im-asha chi ho Chahta i nan-vlhtuka vhleha hvt yukachi tok ;

Atuko yakohmishke, Stephen Belvin achi kash nan-vlhpisa kobafi tuk yvmmak osh inli ka Yunatit Stets im ulhtihkot Paris ahikiyaka nan-ai-im-vlhpisa chi ho yukachi, yohmi kvt 1866 Choliti tuba tok Atikvl 38 ka ik-holitoplo, micha Belvin achi kash micha Chahta okla nan-isht imia-vlhpiesa aiena ka nan-isht ikahnoshke :

Yakahmishke, anumpa yvmma hoyulba fehna ho, Kapetani Joe Everidge, Turner Everidge, micha Martin Everage aiena kvt, nahullo achvffa Luther, yvmmvt itihalvlli hosh sitisin atoko vbi tok osh anumpa isht ai-onotoyulvt, yukvt Yunatit Stets i kot Paris, Texas ahikiya ka afoka tok osh, nan-atak-lvmmi vt Ban ai-inutaka hosh hielishke :

Akma, yakohmishke, Aktoba 30, 1877 micha Aktoba 28, 1889 nan-vlhpisa tohomba tok mako ai-iyakaya hosh Joe Nale Tobaksi Kaunti i Shalif osh nan-vlhpisa ai-im-issa, micha hatak vpi-homa U. S. nan-isht im vtta vt im-ahni hatuk mako Tamaha Krebs C. N. okla aiachvff keyu nah-vlhpisa asanali vhleha-micha nan-vlhpisa keyu bo nan-isht ai ahanta tuk putta ka, in chuka kaniohmi ka kvnchi tok oke ;

Yohmi-ma okla aiachvffa keyu vhleha hvt chuka iyvlii micha nan-imai-okpolokatuk aiena kvt Joe Nale a U. S. Kot Mushkoki ahikiya ka afohoki tok ;

Yakohmishki, Adelphus Riddle vt Mick Nichols iti-halvlli osh Chahta okla ai-iba-chvffa osh Jacks Fork Co., ai-ahanta tuk osh illi tok, yohmi-na yvmma nanah immih hatuk isht ahanta chi (administrator) vlhtoka tuka, Huggins, Arkansas ulhti vtta osh anumpa isht ai-onochit Mushkoki Kot a isht ona tuk oke; Yohmi-na illi tok nan-immi achi kash Kot achi kash yukachit Adolphus Riddle ibbak ai-imakoffit eshi cha illi achi kash ahalaya kvt nan-isht ikania chito ho isht tahpalat kunchi kut, Chahta i kot nan-isht ai-ahanta he aiulhpiesa tuk a nayuhmi isht ikahno ;

Mihma yakohmishke, Sam Harris ut Sam Brown Chahta ai-iba-chuffa uk-inli; micha itatuklo kut County aiahashwa yatuko-itim-okpolokut ahanta cha ubi tok, yohmi ka Chuch Parker Ft. Smith binili kutMorris Green micha inla ai-itapeha Gains County minti kut anumpa yumma chomi ho "nena ka apesa tok a" Chahta okla i kot ako nan-isht imai-asha he ut ai-ulhpisa kut isht otani fehnashke ; Atuko yakohmishke, Sam Harris a Yunatit Stets ut nan-im apesa he ahnit Paris, Texas attuma ahalulli-shke ;

YOHMI HOKA.

Chahta okla i nan-apesa itanahut chieyaka, yakohmit ulh-pissashke. Chahta okla i Miko chito ut ayohma he ut imai-ulhpiesa cha Guthridge, Fleming ai-itapeha Paris Texas aiahash-wa ka tohno-na kot achi kash ont ahoyokut micha kaniohmi hosh anumpa yumma chohmi putta ka, isht utta he imai-ulhpiesa ke-yu ka, isht anumpahonlit, keyukmut Chahta okla micha ai-achu-ffa uhleha aiena nan-isht imai-ulhpiesa ai-ilaiyukali micha Caoli-ti aiena ka apehpoa-hanchashke; Micha nan-isht ahanta tuk isht imulhtuba ka, nana ka ai-imulhtuba he ut ulhpisa tuk osh Miko chito a imotaiyani hokma, satifikit ima ho Tuli-holiso $1500.00 osh ; nan-isht ulhpisa keyu Tuli-holisso sholi ibbak fayuka tuk ut isht ulhtubashke, Nan-ulhpisa ilupput hlopuli mak-inli hosh holitoput itoyulashke.

Ai-okpuchi Nofimba 14, 1889.

BILL LV.

Kaunti i nan-ulhtuka isht im-ulhtuba imi-bafuki nan-ulhpisa.

Chahta okla i nan apesa itanahut chieyaka yakohmit ulhpi-sashke.

Chahta yakni, Kaunti i nan-ulhtuka uhleha isht im-ulhtuba imi-bafuka kut yakohmashke

Kaunti Chuch,	**$100 00**
Kaunti Klak,	**50 00**
Shalif, micha apeluchi, aiyukali,	**50 00**

Tvli-holisso yakohmi kvt isht im-vlhtuba im-issat vlhtaha yvmmako ibafvka-hashke.

Nan-vlhpisa ilvppvt hlopulli mak-inli hosh holitopvt itoyulashke.

Ai-okpachi November 14, 1889.

BILL LVI.

Shalif vt okla ai-achvffa keyu vhleha holhtina esha he nan-vlhpisa toba tok, masholichi nan-vlhpisa.

Chahta okla i nan-apesa itanahvt chieyaka, yakohmit vlhpisashke.

Shalif vt okla ai-achvffa keyu vhleha holhtina esha he Nov. 6, 1888, nan-vlhpisa tobvt holitopa tok vt, himak a mosholashke.

Nan-vlhpisa ilvppvt hlopulli mak-inli hosh holitopvt itoyulashke.

Aiokpache Nofimba 15, 1889.

B. F. SMALLWOOD, P. C..C. N.

BILL LVII.

Chanta okla i holisso apisa ai-imma nan-vlhpisa.

CHAPTA I.

SEKSHVN 1. Nanithvna nan isht imasha.

Chahta okla i nan apisa ittafvmat chiya kat yakmihchit apisashke.

Chahta okla nan ithvna nan isht atta yvt, illvppak atukma isht atobvt hielashke. Yohmi kvt mika chito ak osh miko hatukmakosh yamma pehlichit binilashke, micha holisso apisa i noshkoboka yvt vchvffakma, ulhtih chulasti vt tuchenashke, ulhtih tvloha ka vchvffa aiuka hosh ai vlhtukashke nan apesa aboha ittatuklo kvt ittibaithvnahvt chieya hosh holisso apisa i noshkoboka micha ulhtih chvlasti vhleha aiena kv atokolashke, Yohmi na yammak okvt nan vlhtukvt hieli vfvmmi tuklashke micha vlhtomba chi kvt vlhtukvt im vlhtaha hokmakashke, Yohmik mvt vfvmmi aiukali ka nan vlhtuka isht im vlhtoba, yakohmi aiuka ho okla ishashke, holisso apisa i noskoboka yvt tulli holisso tvhlepa hvnnali ho ishashke, yohmik mvt ulhtih chulasti ʋhleha hʋt tʋlli holisso tʋhlepa nshta a̱ina ai uka ho̱ ishit oklashke, yohmi kʋt hʋshi tuchena a̱ukakma ittakʋshkoa neshʋn i̱ tʋlli holisso akucha hosh imʋlhtobashke.

SEK. 2. Holisso apisa i̱ noshkoboka micha, micha ʋlhtih chulasti ʋhleha aiena kʋt, nanʋlhpisa ʋt nana ho̱ isht aiaha̱shwa chi ho̱ miha putta, ka̱ aia̱lhi cha chi̱ ilekahli kʋt tʋlli holisso tʋhlepa Sipokni tʋhlapi, micha atoni ʋt tuklo ka̱ ola keyu ho̱ ban atukma Chahta neshʋn a̱ imatahli na mi̱ko chito ʋt im aiokpʋchi hokmakashke, Yohmik mʋt ʋchʋffa aiukali kʋt Chahta okla i̱ nan ʋlhtuka ʋleha hʋt anumpa kʋllo ishi chatuk mako̱ ishit oklashke.

SEK. 3. Nan ithʋna nan isht imasha ʋhleha im isht hla̱mpko, micha im atoksʋli aiena kʋt, Yakohmi ai ukali kakashke:

1. Chahta okla i̱ holisso apisa ai imma ka̱ pehliechit afanalihinchashke.

2. Ilap isht imai ʋlhpiesa, micha ʋlla nakni holisso apisa micha ʋlla tek holisso apisa, chukka lokoli kolisso apisa aiena kʋt isht imai ʋlhpiesa nan ʋlhpisa ho ikbashke, Yohmi kia nan ʋlhpisa illʋppak okʋno, ai i̱sʋnali keyu ho̱ ikbashke.

3. Illʋppa iyakaiya makosh holisso pisachi putta ai imomaka pisa hosh atokolashke.

4. Holisso apisa hochito pehlichi ʋhleha ya̱ nanitimapesa, Yohmi kia nan itimʋlhpisa illʋppa chomi ka miko chito yʋt aiokpʋchi micha nan ithʋna isht asha ʋhleha yʋt tuchena ona hosh hochifo takohlichi hokmako̱ holitopashke.

5. Holisso pisachi kʋnima kia okishko hokma, keyukmʋt ikiaʋlhpeso hokma holisso pisacha chi satifikit imʋlhtaha tuk a̱ im ishashke.

6. Holisso apisa putta kʋt holisso kʋniohmi ho̱ pisʋt nan aiithʋna he ya imatokolashke.

7. Abeka lawa keyukmʋt ililli itimʋlmola hinla imma hosh a̱sha hokmʋt ʋlla nakni holisso apisa keyu hokmʋt ʋlla tek holisso apisa hokia yukuplicha he ʋt imaiʋlhpiesashke.

8. Yohma he yʋt aiʋlhpesa ka yimmi̱ hokmʋt chukka lokoli holisso apisa kʋnima kia issacha he ʋt imaiʋlhkpisashke.

9. Yohmi hokmako̱ nanithana kʋt isht ahlampkot i̱ Shalichit maha̱ya hinla ka̱ yimmi hokmʋt chukka lokoli holisso apisa yʋt a hiola he ya̱ imatokʋlashke. Anumpa tʋptoa 8 micha 9 kʋt

nana ahanchi illvppak okvno, ulhti chulasti vhleha akbano kia, yammihcha he vt im aivlhpiesashke.

10. Holisso apisa hiohli putta ka holisso pisvt ai-asha kvt kvnimihchit isht aimahaya chi ka imapesashke, micha yohma he vt imai-vlhpiesacha vlla nakni holisso apisa hiohli hokono yammohmah he vt kvnimak fehna ai-vhlihcha hinla hokmvt, nana ikbi micha nana hokchi ittatuklo illvppvt im vlhvchi micha abachit pihinsa he aiena ka im aiahni cha imapesashke.

11. Neshvn vt attobi vt Stet anukaka ya holisso pisvt ilhkola chi ka atokolashke vlla holisso pisa illvppa chohmi hokono aiyowa kvt holisso apisa hochito hiohli ka holisso apisvt aiasha kako ai ayowvt atokolashke, micha vlla holisso pisa vlhpesa kvt, ulhtih taloha ka, holhtina kvniohmi hosh ai asha ka, nan-isht ithaiyana hosh atokolashke vlla nakni micha vlla tek vt ittilanwashke, micha holisso apisa i noshkoboka ak osh. alikchi impuna ho tohno na yammvt vlla holisso pisvt ilhkola chi hosh vlhtuka kash putta ka afanalichit pesa na vlla yammak ash kvnimatiksitopo yatuk achini hokmvt. Yammak atuk vno kuchechi cha inla ho attobichit ibafvkashke.

Nan-ithvna nan-ish im asha yvt isht i chuwa (seal) osh itoyolashke isht i chuwa yamma holisso lvppali.

BOARD OF EDUCATION, CHOCTAW NATION.

Achi hosh lvpalashke, yammak okvt itanahvt chieya hosh nan-isht asha putta holisso ho ikbit ieshashka yohmi cha nanvlhtuka hatukmak osh holisso nana ho atahli putta ka im isht ichuwa yatukma isht atokolashke.

SEK. 1. Chahta yakni ai anukaka ka himonasi holisso apisa hiohli micha himak pilla ma vlhtaha chi ai ukali ka nan-ithvna nan isht im asha vhleha hvt, holisso apisa pehlichi vchvffa micha holisso pisachi vt tuklo ka takla keyu ho im atokola he vt im ai-vlhpiesashke, yammak achi kvt holisso apisa pehlichi micha holisso pisachi yvt nana-isht ahanta he putta micha nan ithvna kvt kvnima ont ai vhli hokmako tohna hinla, micha kvniohmi hosh isht im vlhtoba he putta ka anowachi hosh, stet ilayuka tuchena takla keyu ho ai-anukaka ka holisso nananoli ya takalichashke, micha Chahta yakni ai-anuka ka ya holisso nan anoli vchvffa ho takali chashke, holisso pisachi vhleha illvppvt holissopisachit ahanta tuk a ufumoni pokoli ka ona micha holısso pisachi impuna, hatak aiulhpisa aiena ka isht ulhtukowa ieshashke, yohmikmut holisso pisachi nakni uhleha hut colleage anowa achukma kunima ho nan aiithunut hlopulli tok yohmi cha German, Latin, Klik micha Flanchi im anumpa aiena ho abacha hinla, mikmut ohoyo holisso pisachi uhleha hut nan ai-ithuna chaha i shali kunima keyukmut holisso pisachi ai-ithuna achukma ho nan ai ithunut hlopulli tok osh, micha nahullo anumpa mikmut anumpa inla tuklo aiena ho abuchi hinla hokmakashke yohmi ka nana ayakohma he ahanchi illuppa putta ka ilaieshi hosh holisso pisachi bunut asilhha hohkia, ubanumpa yimmi okmako im issa he ut im i shahlashke, nan-ulhpisa illuppat holitoput ittoyola hayukma mihniakinli ho holisso apisa i noshkoboka yut, yohma he ut im ai-ulhpiesa cha, holisso, apisa hiohli putta ka 1 pehlichchika ai uka ka, holisso ho ikbi hosh imanoawachi kut, Chahta okla himonasi a holisso apisa putta ka halala chi ho nanimapesa putta hatukma himak holisso apisa im ufummi illuppat taiha hokma ont ai uhli hashke ahni ka im-otunichashke, yohmi cha anonti nan-itimulhpisa himona ho ikbashke. yohmi kut ulla nakni holisso apisa micha ulla tek holisso apisa. Keyukmut holisso apisa chaha osh himak pila ulhtaha chi aiena illuppak o nan itimapsa ikbi hokut sekshun illuppa anumpa tapa ammona takali illuppa micha chapta illuppa sekshun tahlapi kako ai yakaiyashke.

Paragraph 2nd : Himonasi okla putta I holisso apisa hiehmaya illuppak okuno, nan ithuna nan isht im asha uhleha hut yakohmashke ahni hokmut imai ulhpiesashke nan ittim ulhpisa yoka ikbi hokmut tikba ka kummichit ittimapesa chatuk akinli chomi ho ikbi kia nanulhpisa iluppa a miko ako aiyakaiya hosh Home mission iksa nan isht imasha ya ittimapesashke, nan ittimapesa he miha illuppuk atukma yammihchi hohkia. Sekshun illuppa anumpa tupa ammona mikmut Chapta illuppa Sekshun tulhapi hokuno ai akaiya keyu hashke, Yohmi cha neshun okut holisso apisa I pehlichi, keyukmut holisso pisachi kunima hohkia imatoba he okuno ik apeso yohmi cha nanittim ulhpisa yamma chomi putta ka anumpa hut afoyuka kut achi kut, kunimapo hohkia, nan ittim ulhpisa atuka mokofa he ahni hokmʋt hʋshi hʋnnali kʋt takanli moma ho itti haklochi tuk okmakashke, nan ittim ʋlhpisa yamma anumpa illʋppʋt afoka keyu hokmʋt nan ittim ʋlhpisa holittoppa keyumakashhe.

SEK. 5. Holisso apisa hiohli ka pehlichi ʋhleha kʋt, hʋshi tuchena ai yuka ka̱, kʋsh kolit imatobit isht maha̱ya kʋt, ʋfʋmmi ʋchʋffa ka tʋlli holisso tʋhlepa auwatuklo ai yuka hosh im ʋlhtobut oklashke, holisso apisa hochito hiohli achi kash, holisso pisachi hiohma̱ya kʋt ʋfʋmmi ʋchʋffa ka tʋli holisso tʋhlepa ontuklo micha pokoli tʋhlapi ka takla keyu hokmʋt, tuhlepa auwatuklo kʋno ontia keyu ho̱, yammak inli ho̱ chomichi hosh okla moma i̱ tʋlli holisso yatukma akucha hosh imʋlhtobashke, holisso apisa pehlichi ʋhleha hʋt nan ʋlhtuka yammak atukma hieli na ʋffʋmmi hʋnalashke micha holisso isht im asha ʋt yammak achi̱ ho holisso ikbi hosh ittimapesashke yohmi kia holisso apisa pehlichi micha holisso pisachi ʋhleha ha anumpa hʋt onotola na holisso apisa nan isht asha ʋhleba ha̱t ʋlhpesa ahnit apesa hokmʋt kuchichashke, yohmi kia anumpa isht ai onuchi, illʋppa chomi putta kʋno, holisso hosh tobʋt ittoyola na nitak nana micha kʋnima ho̱ yammak atuka̱ aponaklochit ai asha chi̱ hokmʋt anumpa onotola ya tikbanli imanowachi na holisso apisa nan isht asha itikba hatukma ai illapihpoacha he ʋt imaiʋlhpiesashke, yohmikma holisso apisa nan isht imasha ʋhleha hʋt moyoma hosh chieyʋt anumpa nana hosh onotoyola hatukokma isht imashashke, yohmi cha holisso apisa nan isht imasha ʋhleha yʋt ushta ona hosh yohma he ahni hosh itti baiʋchʋffa pulla hokmako̱ anumpa itola yammak atukmʋt holitopashke.

SEK. 6. Holisso apisa hochito ya̱ isht apelachachi hosh tʋli holisso ʋlhpisʋt itoyola putta hokʋno, holisso apisa nan isht imasha ʋhleha hʋt imapesa ho̱ holisso apesa pehlichi ʋhleha hʋt auditor yatukma im a hoyo na yammakokʋt, wʋlint atukma imatahli na tʋlli holisso sholi yʋt yakmichi hosh atobashke, yʋhmi kʋt ʋfʋmmi ʋchʋffa aiukali ka September, Nevember, February micha may hʋshi manti amona aiukali ka ittilanwechit Makoshi hosh holisso apisa pehlichi ʋhleha hatukma imatobash ke, yohmi tuko̱ holisso apisa imʋfmmi ʋt ont tayaha ka holisso apisa pehlichi kʋni̱ma kʋt, tʋlli holisso yʋt atampʋt i̱ tonla hokmʋt tʋlli hollisso sholi ako̱ i faliminchke, sekshʋn illʋppʋt hol isso apisa pehlichi nanitimvlhpisa himona putta ka pit halanlashke.

SEK. 7. Chukka lakoli holisso apisa hiohli ka apisa chi bvnna hosh ilepoffi putta ka, holisso apisa nan isht imasha vhleha kvt nan ithana hokma nana ka akostinichi bvnna hosh afanalichit imomakv pisasheke yammak a chi kvno miko chito micha vlhtih chulasti vhleha aiena hokvt inla ho ilatobichit atokola he vt im aiveapesashke, yohmi kvt hatak chahta okla aivchvffi keyu ho atokoli hohkia vlhpesashke, yohmi kia nanvlhtuka vlhtomba illvppvt nan imaiuna hatukosh nan imvmakv pisa illvppa isht ahanta kvt ithana hosh isht ahnta hinla hokmakashke, holisso pisachi bvnna illvppa im momakv pisa kvt, holisso iitim-anumpuli, holissochi ispel miha, nahullo im anumpa abvchi holisso, micha yakni paknaka isht anumpa, nan isht anowa holisso United States nan ishitanowa illvppa fehna kako, micha United States chahta yakni ittatuklo illvppa i nanvlhpiesa i nvshkvboka kaiha illvppa moyoma ka impunna hokma nana; ka aponahlochit akotinichashke, nan im momakv pisa hosh aisha ai-ittintakla yamma ilap akinli hvsh holisso pisachi bvnna vhleha ya holisso apisa nan isht im asha vhleha yvt kvnimihchit imapesashke ulhtih moma ka nan immokv pisa vt ont ahlupullikma holisso pisachi vlhtuka aiukali kvt nan immpunna itti shashulli ka isht anukfilli hosh, vchvfa atukla micha atuchena illvppa imapesashke vchvffa, achi illvppak osh caaha i shahli hashke, holisso pisachi vlhtuka putta ka holisso apisa nan isht imasha vhleha hvt, holhtina kvnimapo ka atokolichi hosh satifikit imatahlashke, holisso pisachi vhleha ya, chukka lokoli kanima ho i lokel chulasti vt etachvflichi tuk okma yammak ash inli ho pit i helechashke, yohmi kia lokel chusti kvnima kvt holisso pisachi bvnna pit chvffichа hetuk vt ik yammohmo ketuk okma, keyukmvt pit chvffichi tuk kia Satifikit a ihlakoffi tuk okma holisso pisa nan isht imasha vhleha hvt hatak vlhpesa Satifikit ishiho chukka lokoli yammak atuka pit i chvfficashke, nan imomaka pisa ahanchi kash illvppvt ulhtih aiyukali ont vfvmmikma isht ai ashashke, illvppa atoksvlit aiasha tukvt holisso apisa nan isht imasha vhleha hvt nitak vchvffak ma tvlli holisso tvhlapi micha howi holhtina kvniohmi ho anoawa tuk mvt kowi vchvffakma sint tvhlapi hosh im vlhtabashke nan imomaka pisa illuppa isht a̱asha ʋfʋmmi ʋchʋffa ai itintakla ka̱ ulhtih ʋch ʋffa ka itʋnahʋt chieya kʋt ʋitak tʋhlapi kʋno ont ikiyo kashke, nan imomaka pisa illʋppa isht ai̱ sia chi̱ nitak nana micha kʋnima aiyukali ai-itafamʋt chieychi kʋt apesa cha, hushi tuchina kʋt a̱sha moma ho̱ Neshʋn illʋppa aianukaka holisso nananʋli kʋnima ho̱ anowaʋachi makosh holisso ikbit fokashke yohmi tuk osh holisso apisa i̱ nʋshkoboka, nan ʋlhtuka isht apelʋchitʋlli aolisso ibbak fo̱ka yammako̱ akuchit isht atobashke.

SEK. 8. Okla putta I holisso apisa ʋfʋmmi aiyuka li ka Septimba manti amona kako isht-iyashke, yohmi̱ tuk mʋk chun hashi nitak pokoli micha pokoli tuchena ai itintakla ho̱ ont yukopʋt isht maha̱yashke, holisso apisa i̱ nosh koboka micha ulhtih chulasti tuchena hokʋt ʋfʋmmi ai̱yuka holisso pisa tok, nanithʋna tok imomaka pisʋt ai asha ka holisso apisa ai yukoli ai ahashwa he ʋt im ai-ʋlhpiesashke, yakohma chi̱ ka nan-ithʋna nan-isht im asha ʋhleha hʋt yakohmi hokmak osh, micha nitak nana ho̱ ʋlhpesa a̱hnit apesa kʋt holisso apisa i̱ noshkoboka micha ulhtih chulasti ʋhleha aiena kʋt ataklama hosh ona he ʋlhpesa ho̱ apesa tuk osh ilap fehna kʋt nan-ithʋna tok imomaka pisʋt ai-ashashke.

SEK. 9. Holisso apisa putta i̱ noshkoboka yʋt ʋfʋmmi aiyukali ka, tʋlli holisso tʋhlepa ushta pokoli tʋhlapi osh holisso apisa imma ho nana kʋt isht a kʋnia he osh ibbak fo̱kashke, yohmikma ulhtih chulasti ʋhleha hʋt tʋlli holisso tʋhlepa ontuklo pokoli tʋhlapi osh ibbak i̱ fokashke, yohmi tuk mʋt kʋnimichi tuk putta kʋt, nan-ithʋna he imma nan-isht im asha ʋt ʋtʋmmikma itafamʋt chieyakma ʋlhtukowa ka imtoni̱chashke nana chini̱poa ho nan-isht a kʋnia hinla asha kia nan-ʋlhpisa ʋt yamma ik atahlo tok a putt ka a̱sha hokma iskʋli nan isht atoba he osh ibbak fo̱ka tok illʋppak asho̱ akuchat isht ʋlhtobashke.

SEC. 10. Nan ithʋna he nan-isht im asha ʋhleha hokʋt ʋfʋmmi ʋchʋffa ka himona hokono itʋfahamashke, yohmi kʋt Tʋshka Homa ako ai-itafamashke yohmi kʋt nan apesa itafama tuk nitak hu̱llo ʋchʋffa amona yamma ai-iti̱ta̱kla ho nan ithʋna nan isht im asha yokʋt itafamut chieyashke yohmi cha ʋfʋmmi yamma anu̱ka̱ka. Nan a kʋniohmi tok nan anowa he putta imasha tuk mʋt report atukma nana pesa chieya ka i̱ bohlashke, yohmi ka nan anowa bohli yammak okʋt, holisso apisa imma nana kuniohmi ho iskulli a isht atobit isht mihinti tok putta ka uchafohlichit takolichi hashke yohmi ka nan ithuna nan-isht imasha ut moma kak atuk okma keyu hokmut yamma ai-uchuffa kunima hosh hatak putta ka otonichashke, yohmikmut nan anowa holisso yammak okut ufummi ant ahlupulli ka kuniohmi putta ka utonichashke, yohmikmut nan ithuna kut i shalit iya a kuniohmi micha holisso putta ont pihisa tok micha anonti nana kut yakohmi hokmut i shala hinla ahni tok putta hokut nan ithuna nan isht imasha illuppat yohma he ulhpesa ahni aputta hokut nan apisa oka yakohmi hokbano ahnit anumpa im ahe ut imai-ulhpesashke yohmi kut nan ithuna nan isht imasha illuppak okut ilap nan isht asha tok anowa holisso ha micha holisso apisa pehlichi aiyuka nan anowa holisso ikbi tok putta ma aianichit, nan apesa okla hoka i bohlashke.

SEK. 11. Nan ithuna isht imasha i noshkoboka ut a yohma he ulhpesa ahni hokmut nan-ithuna isht asha oka itafumicha he ut im ulhpesa yohmi kut kunimako yammak ahinla ahnit atokoli tok ma ai itafama he oke.

HOLLISSO APISA I NOSHKOBOKA.

CHAPTA II.

SEKSHUN 1. Holisso apisa putta i noshkoboka ak osh, nan ithun nan isht imasha oka i nan ulhpisa ahlichi nan ulhtuka mak ash i hikia cha nana ho apesa tuk micha anumpa nana hosh yakohmashke ahnit nan ithuna nan isht imasha achi kash osh aiyakaiya chi hosh apesa tuk putta ma nan ai-ahni yammak ai ahlichit isht mahayashke.

SEK. 2. Yohmikmut Chahta ulla uhleha hut Chahta yakni hashakucha ya holisso ont apisut ai asha putta, i noshkoboka hiohli putta micha ulla, okla putta immi yo nan isht ithuna osh maya putta ma holisso itimut nan ithunut mahaya micha a buna putta ma im akostinichi achukmashke.

ULHTIH CHULASTI.

CHAPTA III.

SEKSHUN 1. Ulhtih chulasti ai yukali kut holisso isht i chuwa okut nan isht im ai utta atukma itoyolashke, yohmi hosh holisso isht i chuwa yamma uhli ha anumpa hut; Choctaw Nation

District Trustee, achi hosh takalashke yohmikma a fulota ulhtih ai ahunta yammut Chahta i hohchifo nana hokmut yammak takalikma District achi hosh takalashke, ulhtih chulasti okut ulhtukut anumpa kullo putta im ulhtaha mak-inli hosh holisso Tulli holisso sholi ut ibbak toka yamma ilap hohchifo ha i takalichahe o holisso yammut ibbak foyokashke yohmi cha nan ulhpisa mika pulla ho ulhtih chulasti ut holisso satifikit ikbi putta hokut ilap hohchifo ha ilap fehna hosh takalechicha i holisso isht i chuwa atukma lapalihinchashke.

SEK. 2. Chukka lokoli holisso apisa o holisso pisachi ulhcha hokut ulhtih kunima o holisso apisachi tok o anowa holisso atukma atahlik ma lokil chulasti okut isht ulhtukowa anumpa ha atakulechi ho ulhtih chulasti ut hushi uchuffa aiyuka ka holisso Satifikit a ima hokma Chahta okla moma i tulli holisso sholi akoshatobashke. Yohmik ma ulhtih chulasti uhleha hokut holisso pisachi nan anowa holisso ikbi na anumpa ahli achi mut ulhtaha tok putta hosh ibbakfoka hokut achukmalit itahobi tok osh ilapo ut imai ulhtih nan isht anowa holisso ikbit nan ithuna isht asha ut ufummikma itafamut chiayakma yamma ai inichit bohlashke.

SEK. 3. Ulhtih chulasti uhleha hokut, nan ithuna isht asha okut ont ufummi itunaha ulhpisa itafamut chieyakma, ulla holisso pisa uhleha hohchifo, putta ka lokil chulasti ut imatahali toka, nan ithuna isht asha atukma im anowacha chaske.

SEK. 4. Ulhtih chulasti uhleha hut ayohma he ut imai ulhpisesacha, chukka lokoli kunima ka momut abeka hokma, keyukmut ililli itimulmoli osh itonla hokma, nana hokma holisso pisa ya yokobli cha he ut imai ulhpiesashke.

SEK. 5. Ulhtih chulasti ai yukali kut ilap im ai ulhtih akinli, ka holisso pisachi, kunima ka anumpa hut isht ai onotola ho, anowa ka anumpa ishi hokmut ushalika fehna makinli i Siilhhichit pisa pullashke, anumpa isht aionotula kash ut ahli pullakma, hatak yukuplechi cha, anonti holisso pisachi inla kut, nan ithuna isht imasha itikba onut holisso pisacha he ona hosh holisso ishi tuk ut bikia hokma yammako atobechi na holisso apisa yammak ash, holisso pisachashka.

CHAPTA IV.

SEKSHUN 1. Chukka lokoli putta kut hatak chukka

uchuffa i noshkoboka o ulhtih chulasti imai ulhtih ai anukaka ai atokoli ho lokil chulastiut holisio pisa he uffummi anukaka lokil chulasti ulhtukut hielashke.

SEK. 2. Lokil chulasti ut chukka lokoli ai ahanta yamma, Chahta ai uchuffa keyu hohkia holisso pisacha he ona pulla kut anta hokma yammak holisso pisachachi ho imomaka pisa ut imaiulhtih yammak inli ka ufummik ma itafamut ashakma pit chufichashke, Yohmikmut lokil chulasti yammak okut, hushi uchuffaema himona hokuno holisso apisa ya i nowut pisa pullashke, micha hushi uchuffa holisso pisachi tuk holisso o, nan anowa yammak ma afanalichit apusiiachit ulhpesa hokma anumpa ahli i takalichi aiena he ut imai ulhpiesashke, yohmik ma holisso pisachi tok u aheka toba yammak ash micha aiahli anumpa atakali tok yammah ash holisso pisachi akinli hosh ulhtih chulashti a pit imahe at imai ulhpiesashke, Yohmik mut lokil chulasti uhleha hokut holisso pisachi, kunima kut anumpa onotola hokma ai i Silhha he micha nan illuppa afoyoka, ka iyakaiut ulhtih chulasti oka imanowachashke. Yohmikmut lokil chulasti uhleha hokut holisso pisachi uhleha, hut i holisso apisa ulla aiasha ka akuniohma he nan ulhpisa i toula kut ai alichi ka holisso pisa uhleha hokut, holisso pisachi a im antia holitobli, aiena chi ka achukmalit nan imoktubli achukmashke.

SEK. 3. Lokil chulasti uhleha hut nan ulhtoba nan 'kia ik sho ho toksulashke.

SEC. 4. Lokil chulasti uhleha hukut ilap i chukka lukoli aiyukali ka ulla ufummi ontuklo micha auwa-cntuchona ont ai uhli ka hohchifo a ishit holisso afukit tahlicha, yammak atukma ulhtih chuiasti oka holisso pisa im u fummi ut ont tahakma im otunichashke.

CHUKKA LOKOLI HOLISSO APISA.

SEKSHUN. 1. Chukka lokoli kunima hohkia holsso pisachi a tohna hinla hokmut holisso apisa ut i hikiashke, yammak okuno yohmi kia holisso apesa hiohli kut itibilika kut kowi tuchena aianukka kuno keyu kashke yakni kowi ulhpisa kut hina chito itti chunulli anowa y osh apisali achukma ai apesashyammak okunu yohni akinli kia tamaha ahni ho talaya hokuno kowi ulhpisa yammut isht ik imoktublokasko yohmi kut nan ɒlhpisa illɒppa afoyoka kɒt chapta 1st anum tɒptoa 8 micha 9, mikmɒt Sekshɒn 3 nan ithɒna isht asha imma ɒt nau isht a̱hli im issa takali kako aiyakaiyashke.

SEK. 2. Chukka lokɒli holisso apisa poyutta hokɒt ɒfɒmmi aiyuka ka Siptimba minti ɒmmona kako isht aiashke, yɒhmik mɒt nitak aiyu̱kali ka kɒshi kɒnalli hɒnali ho phi̱sashke nitak hullo aiena hokono keyu kashke, nitak moma ka hoshi kɒnnlli kɒnima ho holisso hapisɒt isht iya mikmɒt ont afoha he aiena kɒt apesashke yamohmit maha̱ya hosh may hɒshi nitak ont isht aiopi kako̱ ont im ai ɒlhlashke amba ulhtih chulasti ɒt ahni hokmɒt holisso apsia yohmi ka nitak falaya keyu kia fohachashke.

SEC. 3. Chahta ɒlla poyotta hokɒt chahta yakni anukaka holisse apisa i̱ kɒnia keyu hosh nanithɒna he imissa ahli kɒt chahta ɒlla ahli yammak ila hoke yohmi hoka himak pilla mahaya ka ɒlla Iki ishke I̱ kiatin ɒhleha aiena kɒt holisso apisa yohmi kako̱ tihlehinli pullashke.

SEC. 4. Ɒlla putta holisso pisa chi̱ ho̱ hohchifo ɒt holisso afoka tok putta kɒt ik ai̱ahlo hokma ɒlla yamma i̱ki keyukmɒt atoni aiena kɒt holisso pisa he tuk nitak i̱ kɒnia putta ka̱ nitak ɒchɒffak ma sint pokolit iya ho̱ atoba he ɒt onɒtola cha atobashke, yohmi kia nan ɒlhtoba onotolɒt atoba he illɒppɒt hɒshi ɒchɒffa ka tɒlli holisso tuklo keno ont iya keyu kashke amba ɒbeka, kucha okpullo keyukmɒt ayohma he fehna ho nana ka isht ataklama hatuk okmɒno keyu kashke, iskɒli atoba he achi kɒt nan ɒlhpisa illɒppa chapta VI micha sekshɒn 5 tɒhlapi miha taka li kako̱ aiyakaiya hashke nan ɒlhtoba he isht anumpa takali illɒppak okɒt kaunti tɒlli holisso akokɒno i̱kɒniiohmikia ik akucho kashke amba ulhtih kɒnima hatukma yamma i̱ chulasti ako ibbɒk fokashke, yohmi cha iskɒli' ɒt ibbɒk foka cha akɒni mihcha he nan ɒlhpiasa ɒt imissa tuk yammak o̱ ai-ibafokashke ulhtih chulasti okɒt yohma he ɒt ɒlhpisa fehna hokma ɒlla kɒnuma ka nitak lawa, keyu ka holsso apisa foha chi̱ ka imissa he ɒt im ai ɒlhpisashke.

SEK. 5. Chukka lokoli holisso pisachi ɒhleha hɒt ɒlla ɒchɒffa holisso pisachi kɒt hashi ɒchɒffak ma tɒlli holisso tuklo hosh im ɒlhtobashke yohmi ka̱ ɒlla yɒt hɒshi achɒffa yamma holisso pihinsa na nitak pokoli tuklo ka ontia hokma, amba yamma ona keyu hokmɒno nitak ɒchɒffak ka sint pokolit iya ho̱ im ɒlhtobashke, yohmi akinli kia holisso pisachi itishasholi kvt chaha i̱ shahli amona kvt tvlli holisso pokoli ushta akucha tvhlapi ontia keyu ho imvlhtobashke, yohmikmvt atukla kvt tvlli holisso pokoli tuchena ontia keyu hosh imvlhtobashke yohmikma ont atuchena kvt tvlli holisso pokoli tuklo ontia keyu hosh imvlhtobashke.

SEK. 6. Holisso pisa vt hashi micha nitak nana ho hikit iya tokma hashi iyaka̱ya ka nitak atuka̱ ont ohmi hokmako hashi vchvffa isht vlhpisashke.

HOLISSO APISA HOCHITO.

CHAPTA VI.

SEKSHVN 1. Holisso api̱sa hochito putta i̱ pehlichika Chahta yakni anukaka ya, holisso apisa pehlichit ahanta chi kvt, nan isht ilekahli (Bond) o̱ hatak tuklo kono takla keyu hosh apelachit atoni tvlli holisso tvhlepa sipokni tahlapi isht ileonuchit Mi̱ko chito ya im atahli na̱ ai-okpvchi hashke, yohmi kvt nana ho isht ai-ahanta he a̱ nan vlhpisa hvt miha mikmvt nan-ithana nan isht im asha nan itimapesa tok aiena ka ai ahlichit ai yakaiyvt ahanta chi makashke.

SEK. 2. Holisso apisa pehlichi vlhleha hokvt holisso yamma chohmi ai yukali ka ishi cha nan isht ahanta kvt, nan ithvna nan isht imasha vhleba hvt nana ho̱ apihi̱sa tok ma mihyo ahlichit isht ahanta shke. Yammohmi tok osh holisso pisa im vfvmmi vt ont taiyahakma nan vlhtukoa anowa ka nan ithvna nan-isht im asha atukma im anowaha̱nchashke, nan anowa holisso yamma chohmi vlla holisso pisa hohchifo micha vfvmmi kvniohmi, micha nan ithvna kvt kvniohmi, mikmvt nana inla micha holisso apisa i̱ nan-vlhpisa ma kvniomit inutakvt hilli a̱ putta mikmvt nana ho̱ chumpa ho iskvli vt kvnia tok a̱ achafolechi hosh takohlichit tvlli holisso kvniohmi hosh ibbvk foka tok micha kvniohmi ho kanchi tok putta mikmvt aheka atobi tok holisso putta ma, moyoma ka̱ nan ithvna isht im asha atukma imanowaha̱nchashke.

SEK. 3. Ulla holisso pisa.

Holisso apisa Spencer Academy a̱ vlla nakni osh tvhlepa vchvffa hashke, mikmvt New Hope a̱ vlla tek osh tvhlepa vchvffa bika hosh Chahta Chikisha i̱ yakni ai asha ka a kuchvt holisso apisa illuppa iyashke yohmikma pokoli chakali akucha chakali, bika ho, nan ithuna isht im asha, okut, Chahta yakni kaunti tuloha ai okali ka yohmi ho tehlelashke, ahnit imapesashke, yohmikmat nan ithuna nan isht im asha illuppak ash ot holisso pisut iya chi ka nittak pokoli tuchena kut takali moma ho Kaunti Judge uhleha ha im anowa chi kut ulla nakni micha ulla tek aiena kut kuniohmi ai yuka hosh i kaunti a akuchit iya chi ka im otunichashke, yohmikma kaunti chuch ash ot chukka lokoli holisso apisa atok ai yukali i tokolichit ai aowashke yohmikmut holisso imma kut iki uhleha keyumut, atoni uhleha hako holisso satitikit a imashke.

SEK. 4. Ulla yohmi kut holisso apisa ya ik chukowo kisha ka yammak asho holisso apisa pehlichi ut atokoli tok o anta tok ulikchi impuna ut yammak osh ulla yammut hak-nip achukma akuniohmi ka afanalichit pisashke, yohmikmut nan ithuna hinla im anukfila akuniohmi ka yakohmi hokmak osh, ulhpesa binla ahnit nan ithuna nan isht imasha ut tok aiena ka ai akaiyut afanalichit pihi-sashke, ulla yut ufummi akok uto isht im oktapo kashke yohmi kia nan ithuna he ai-ulhpesa kut ufummi tuhlapashke yohmi kia ulla kuniohmi kut ufummi falaya ishahli kia anta he holisso apisa pehlichi ut kucha hokbano ahnit nan ithuna isht asha yamma im anowachi ho keyu kuchi ho hokmut.

SEK. 5. Kaunti Chuch uhleha ut ulla holisso pisa, chi ho atokilichit aiowa to putta hohchifo micha kunima ho holisso ha ai ishi hatuk aiena holisso apisa okla putta immi yamma hikia ka i pehlichi a imotunichaske mikmut Shalif kaunti yamma anta hochifo micha i holisso ai itola aiena ka ainichit imanowachaske, yohmi tuk o ulla holisso pisa iya chi tuk a holisso apisa ut tiwa tuk a nitak pokoli ontia keyukmut holisso apisa ut tiwa hayatuk o holisso ha ishi tuk okma nitak pokoli ona micha holisso apisa i pihlichi ot im annowa tuka nittak pokoli ona ho ulla yammak ashot holisso ap isa ya ont ikhayako hokma holisso apisa i pehlichi ut a yohma he ut im aiulhpiesa cha Shalif kaunti yamma anta ka imanowachashke, yohmik ma Shalif okut usha lika fehna ho kuniohmi ho holisso apisa ya ikiyo hatukma akostinichit pisashke, Yohmi cha ulla ut ilap fehna kak osh abeka, keyukmut i chukka achuffa kunima hosh abeka keyukmut Bok hofobi ho isht ataklama hokma nan keyu hatuk o akoshtinichi hokmut yammak atuk o nitak tuhlapi ka takla ho ulla yammak ash holisso apisa kunima ho iya hetuk a ont bohlashke, yohmi kut Shalif yammut yakohmit nowut ayut nan isht i kunia putta hokuno ulla yamma Iki keyukmut atoni aiena kak osh atobashke,yokmi ka atoksuli illuppak o Shalif ut aya hokuto nitak uchuffak ma tulli holisso tuklo ho imulhtubak mut kowih achuffakma sint tuhlapi hosh imulhtobashke, Yohmi kut atiya he ulhpesa pit apisali hina iya pullashke, yohmi cha Shalif ash ot nowut aya tuk nitak kuniohmi tok aienma anumpa kullo isht onotula hosh aheka ya ulla Iki atoni atuk aiena ka ibolashke, yohmi kia ulla Iki keyukmut atoni atuk ash osh atobi ik buno hokma ulhtih yamma i sakit kot itikba ya aheka yammak atuka isht onacha, chuch nana ahli ka ont im otunichi hokma, yohmi kut nana akumniohmi ho aheka ut toba tok putta ka imotunichi, micha iskuli lawa kuniohmi mikmut nan isht ataklama nan isht i kunia aiena im otunichi hokma himak a chakalichit ulla Iki kayukmut atoni aiena ka ik hoyo kia chuch yammut ulhtoba pulla. chi ka apesa, yohmi tok kia nan apesa kush ikimaiahlo hokma yohmi hokma kaunti i tulli holisso sholi ut aheka ontola yammak ash ut kaunti kunima ho utta atukma yamma i tulli holisso sholi ut Shalif a imatobashke yohmi kut kaunti chuch okut ahek ahli micha ai ulhpesa pulla ahni hokma micha haunti nana atobi yammak okut shalif nan imulhtoba he ash holisso nan isht ai ahli o kot ut apesa tok o ieshi hosh aheka yammut im ulhtoba he im ai ulhpiesa atuk a ulhtobut aheka yamma ieshashke kaunti yammak inli ka ulla uchuffa ka atampa hosh holisso apisa iya he tuk ut ikahlo kut asha hokma Shalif yammak okut mominchit himona uchuffa isht iyashke. Yohmi kia Sakit Kot kunima hohkia nan ulhpisa illuppa nana miha putta kako ai i yakaiya ho aheka ut isht atoba tok o keyu hokuno ulhtoba he ik apesokashke.

SEK. 6. Hatak chukkachvffa kunima hohkia hommona uchuffali ka ulla ya tuklochit chahta i yakni holisso apisa hochito hiohli kak okma. keyuumut nahullo i yakni okma nana ka okla putta i tulli holisso osh ulhtoba chi ho ikbohle kashke.

ULLA ULHTAKLA HOLISSO APSA.

SEKSHUN. 1. Ulla nakni pokoli tuhlapi hosh Armstrong

Academy a aiashashke yohmik ma ulla pokoli talhapi hosh Wheelock holisso apisa ya aiashashke yohmi tuk osh holisso pisa kut ont foha hohkia ulla ut i kunomi keyukmut i kana aiahli o ont takla anta hinla ka iksho hokma holisso apisa pehlichi akinli kak osh pehlichit apesachashke.

SEK. 2. Ulla ulhtakla okuto im ufummi ai imma kako isht imoktupa kut ikshokaske, nan ithuna he ut uffummi tuhlapikak ashke amba nan ithuna nan isht imasha akosh ahni hokmut ulla kunimi kut holisso apisa ya ahanta moma he a imahni keyukmut kochicha he ut imaiulhpesashke, ulla holisso pisa nana hohkia na ithuna nan isht asha akosh ahin keyukma holisso apisa ya ikkuchecho kashke.

SEK. 3. Nan ithuna isht asha uhleha hut ulla lawa kuniohmi hosh holisso apisa hochito iya he a apesa tok yammak inli ohmi ho kaunti chuch ulhleha hokut ulla a hoyashke yohmi kut ilbasha moma i shahli ako hoyo pullashke, yohmi cha uchuffa ka atampa kia yamma chohmi hokuto chukka uchuffa ya akochashke.

SEK. 4. Yohmikma Shalif ai yukali kut ulla holisso pisa chi illuppa itahubit tahli cha holisso apisa kunima ho iya he ulhpisa tok a isht ona pullashke yohmikmut shalif okut nitak uchuffakma tulli holisso tuhlapi micha nana i kunia tuk intokowa hokuno aheka ai ahli ka kaunti tulli holisso Sholi a imotunichi hokma yammak osh atobashke.

SEK. 5. Ulhtakla holisso apisa pehlechi uhleha hokut, holisso apisa hochito pehlichi ut (Bond) imulhtaha he nan ulhpisa illupput micha tuk yammak inli ho yammihchashke, yohmikmut nan anowa holisso hoka nan ithuna isht asha oka ibohla he atuka yammakinli chohmashke, nan ulhpisa illupput hlopuli hayut holitoput ahlit itoyolashke, yohmikma nan ulhpisa inla kut moma hokma akashapa akanima-hosh nan ulhpisa i sunali holisso apisa aiima akuniohma he aputta ka yohmi hokmut yammut kobafa mak oke.

Aktoba 31, 1890.

Miko ut aiokpuchi tok.

BILL LVIII.

Nan ulhtuka hikia hosh ileok punit ile kalakshi chi, mikmut iskuli yo fot iti-ulichit ahanta tok isht im ahleka he nan ulhpisa.

SEKSHUN 1. Chahta ai uchuffa kunima hosh nan ulhtoka holitopa micha okla hut a yimmi ho nan isht imulhtomba kak osh nan ulhtokut Chahta okla i nan ulhpisa ai anutaka hosh hikia tok, a keyokmut nananoli keyukmut chuli osh Chahta okla i kut o ai uchuffa atok osh ai ulhpisa keyu ho iskuli kuniohmi keyukmut nan osh iskuli a itiulla hinla fehna ho ho ishi keyukmut isha he ut ulhpisa ahni yohmi kut nan-ulhtoka, nan anoli okma keyukmut chuli okma nana kut ulhtukut anumpa kullo a isht imulhtaha ha yosh nana kut illuppak achi ahni ho micha imatoba hinla kut kuna hoh kia imia kut im anuk fila micha nan ulhtuka hikia tok. Nan isht ai utta atuk, yammak o folochit isht ilapelachi hosh, nan anoli, keyukmut chuli okma nana hatuk osh, yohmi tuk mut nan ik ai ulhpeso ahli mako isht ulhpesa cha chuli hochito ut anumpa onuchi na ulhtukowa hokmut nan isht imahleka kut ulhtoba onotola kut tulli holisso tuhlepa uchuffa ola takala keyu ho atobachi kut imulhpisashke, yohmi tuk osh nan atoba he a tukut, ikatobo ho nitak uchuffa kut o shohbi hokmut tuhlepa, uchuffa ka ontia keyu hosh, nalibilka ho onotola achuk mako famashke.

SEK. 2. Chahta okla moma nana atukoli okma keyukmut kuniohmi i tokowa hosh nan atukoli okma nana chi ho Chahta i nan ulhpisa ut miha ho nan atokola he ulhpesa Chahta yakni ai ahanta atukma hatak nana hosh ok poni bunna hosh nana kia iskulli iti ulla he fahna keynkmut oka homi keyukmut iskulli okma nana ho isht haksichi bunna kut yammak atuk mako ilap ahnit fot, i konia he tuk a fololichi bunna hosh micha ilap ai ahni ho fot ima he im ahni hosh yammichi tuk putta kut nan-ulhpisa kobuffi mako isht ulhpesa na chuli hochito ut anumpa onocht na ulhtokawa hokmut nan-ulhpisa illuppa amona takali nan isht im ahleka kuniohmi ahe mia takali kak inli ho isht imahlekashke. Nan ulhpisa illupput hlopulli na ai-okpuchi makinli ho ai ahlit kullot hohtoput itoyolashke.

November 3, 1890, Miko ut ai-okpuchi tok.

BILL LIX.

Nanatokoli isht asha tuk holisso yammvt m_iko chito micha nan vlhtoka hochito putta vlhtuka tok holisso putta kvt ikai okpuloko ka he nan vlhpisa.

Chahta okla nan apesa itvnahvt chieya ka yakohmit vlhpisashke,

SEKSHVN 1. M_iko chito vlhtuka ho̱, nanatokoli poyutta ka keyukmvt nanvlhtuka hochito kvnima keyukmvt moma hosh vlhtuka tok, holisso ha chvch chito kvnima ho imona he vlhpesa ka shalif keyukmvt apelachi kvnima kvt isht imonashke, yohmik ma chuch chito ahanchi kash ot shalif yammvt nan atokoli holisso hohchifo micha akvniohmi hosh ibbvk foka vlhkama achukma keyukmvt ai okpuloka chohmi aputta hokma nana ka vlhtukowa ho̱lisso shalit a imashke.

SEK. 2. Chvch chito ashot nanatokoli holisso yammvt m_iko chito keyukmvt nan vlhtuka hochito inla putta vlhtuka holisso yammvt ibak fokka mak inli hosh itomibi ku̱llo achukma ikokpolo hosh keyukmvt, afoka he vlhpisa ka fokashke, yohmik ma nan inla kia yamma ibafo̱ka keyu amba m_iko chito atokoli keyvkmvt okla moma i̱ nanvlhtuka a̱ atokolit isht ai asha tok holisso yammak ila hosh foyokashke yammohmi ho̱ chvch chito osh holisso hash ot itombi okma keyukmvt afoka he vlhpesa yamma foyoka ho ieshi kvt ashana achukma ho ieshashke. Yohmi tuk osh nitak kvn-ohmi kako̱ holissochi chito ako ibbok foka he a̱ nan vlhpisa hvt miha hatuk mako̱ yamihchashke, Yohmi kvt chvch chito okvt holisso yamma cheyohmi kvt ibbvk foyoka ai vhli kvt hatak nana kia ikpisachokmvt nana hosh kvnio̱hmi hohkia kvna hvt pisa he potvla he aiena ka̱ ik imahnokashke.

SEK. 3. Yohmi tuk osh ont ai vlhpiesakma chvch chito ash ot ilap fehna akinli hosh nan atokoli holisso hash ieshit holissochi chito atukma ibbvk ont fokashke, yohmikma holissochi chito ashot, chvch chito okvt shalif vbleha ha, kvnimichit holisso ai vlhtukowa, ima he miha tuka yamakinli ohmi ho̱ chvch chito holisso kashofa imashke.

SEK. 4. Yammohmi tuk o̱ holissochi chito ash ot nanatokoli holisso hash ibakfokashke, yohmikma anumpeshi vt kʊnimihchit holisso ha ima he achi kash inli ohmi holissochi chito a imas hke.

SEK. 5. Chʊch chito okʊt shalif ʊhleba ha holisso kashofa ima kʊt holbʊt toba ka mihmakinli ka ikbit ishi bano tuk osh, nan atokoli holisso yammak ash, holissochi chito a ibbʊk foki hayokmʊt holisso shalif ima tok holbʊt toba ishi tuk ash ot aboha nakfisb im-anumpeshi a ibbʊk fokashke.

SEK. 6. Chʊch chito kʊnima hokʊt abeka hokma keyukmʊt nan inla kia isht ataklama cha nanatokoli holisso, mikmʊt holisso shalif ʊhleha ha ima tok holba ihsi aiena hoka ilap fehna ash holissochi chito micha aboha nakfisn im-anumpeshi ibbʊk foka he anumpa ʊba takali kʊt im achi kasho, yohma hekeyu hokmʊt nan kʊniohmit aya hekeyu kʊt ashlinka ho holisso chi chito a im-anowachashke yohmikma holisso chi chito ashot ilap fehna hosh. Kʊnima chʊch chito yammʊt ai ʊtta hatuk a iyashke yohmicha nanatokoli holisso micha shalif holisso ima tok holba putta ishi tuka ont im ishashke yohmikmʊt holisso isht ʊlhtakowa imashke yamohmi tuk mʊt nanatokoli holisso micha holisso holba tok ishi tok putta yammak ash o moma ka aboha nakfish anumpeshi a imashke, yohmi kia holissochi chito kʊniohmit nan ʊlhpisa ʊt a kʊniohma he miha tuk a aya he keyu hokma sinit i miko akosh nan ʊlhtoka hochito kʊnima kak osh holissochi chito nana a kʊniohma he a tuka ʊlhtumbʊt iya he a atokolashke.

SEK. 7. Yohmi kʊt nan atokoli i chʊch kʊnima kʊt nan atokoli isht asha tuk holisso hoka satifikit ibbit a takalicha he tuk ʊt ik yohmo keyukmʊt yammano takalichi hohkia kʊnimihchit ʊlhtuka ibbʊk foka he nanʊlhpisa ʊt miha tuk a aiahlichi ikbʊnokit ahanta tuk okmʊt keyukmʊt a kʊnimapo ka ik yohmo tuk okmʊt, nanʊlhpisa kobʊffi ikai ʊlhpeso ai ahli mako isht ʊlhpisat chuli hochito ʊt anumpa anuchi na ʊhltokowa nan isht imahleka onotola kʊt tʊlli holisso tʊhlepa ʊchʊffa kʊno takla keyukmʊt tʊlli holisso tʊhlepa tʊhlapi kʊno ontia keyu ka atoba chi kʊt onotolashke, atuko nan ʊlhtoba onotola tuka, ik atobo nitak ʊchʊffa kʊt taha hokma fʊma pokoli tuchena akʊcha chakkli kʊno takla keyukmʊt tʊhlepa ʊchʊffa ontia keyu hosh inali bieka ho on otola achukma mako fʊmashke.

Nofimba, 13, 1890, Miko ʊt aiokpʊchi tok.

REED LIBRARY
STATE UNIVERSITY COLLEGE
FREDONIA, NEW YORK 14063

BILL LX.

Chahta okla aiʋchʋffa yosh anumpa kʋllo ishit United States ibafoka aiemma.

Chahta yakni i̱ nan apisa ittanahat cheiya kʋt yakmichchit apisashki yohmi kʋt chahta hatak ʋpi homma okla ya̱ aia chaffa yammʋt issish ai imma hosh aiʋchaffa hokma, kiyokmʋt nan ʋlhpisa yosh im issa hʋ aiʋ chaffa hokma kiyokmʋt okloshi a chi kasho̱ ohoyo ai itti halʋli hatok makosh isht ibafoka cha chahta okla i̱ nan ʋlhpisa hatokma i̱ notakʋt ahanta tok osh United States ibafoka kʋt anumpa kullo ishi tok okma kiyokmʋt himak pilla ma anumpa kʋllo yammak atokma ishi hokma, nana hoh kia, chahta okla i̱ nan ʋlhpisa hatakma̱ i̱ notakʋt nan ʋlhtoka nana kia ik isho kashke micha neshʋn ahan chi kash aiano̱ ka̱ ka ya̱ nan atokoli nana hoh kia bot ikim a kʋniyo kashki mecha chata okla i̱ nan ʋlhpisa ai inotaka kot hiohli kʋnima hoh kia chuli ʋlhtokʋt ik binnilokashke nan ʋlhpisa ilappat hlopolli mak inli hosh holitopat ittoyolashke.

Oktoba 25, 1890, Fehna aiokpa chi tok.

BILL LXI.

Hoshok hasha kani pila ai-imma Nofimba 1st, 1882, nan ʋlhpisa tok sikshʋn 2, ya̱ alhpoksia.

Chahta yakni i̱ nan apisa ittʋnahat chi-iya kʋt yakmih chit apisashke yohmi kʋt nan-ʋlhpisa ilappat hlupulli haiyokano oktak hashok okma keyokmat ko̱wi hʋshok nana hohkia kanchi kiyokmat nana isht ittatoba chi hokma nana hosh yakni haiyaka akokma kiyuk mat sitisin i̱ holihta ano̱ka̱ ka yo̱ a̱ bashli hokma nana hoh kia tʋn ʋchʋff akma tʋlli holisso ʋchaffat iya kaʋnti ya imatoba shke, kaonti tʋloha ka shalit hiohli kʋt nan-ʋlhtoba hi ahanchi kasho ittahobi cha i̱lap ʋt tok salitok isht im ʋlhtoba ka̱ tʋlli holisso achaffakma sint pokoli ho̱ a ko chit ishi cha kaonti nana ho̱ hashok abasha tuk okma yamma i̱ kaonti tʋlli holisso shole hik kia hatukma im atoba shki yohmi na kaunti ya̱ isht apila cha shki yohmi kia sitisin nana hosh ilap akinli isht ilapila cha chi̱ hosh hashuk boshli hokono. Nan-ʋlhpisa ilappa isht a̱ mia̱ hosh ʋlhtoba ik onocho kashke nan-ulhpisa ilappat hlupulli mak-inli hosh holitopat ittoyolashki.

October 30, 1890, fihna ai-okpuchi tok.

BILL LXII.

Chahta okla nan-apisa itafamat chi-yaka yakohmit ulhpisashke yohmi kut nipi ka chi Chahta i yakni anokaka hiohlit ai asha kut aba chi hosh chumpa putta kat wak micha shok ha aiena basha micha isht i chowa micha kana ho i chompa apotta kat holisso chit ishi bieka hashki yohme tok osh hashi taha ai-okalikma kaunti kanima ho nipi akanchit ahanta hatok mat kaunti yamma kot i holisso chi a holisso yammak ash ibak fokashke.

SAK. 2. Yamomik ma kaunti kot i holissochi ahliha hokut holisso yohmi ka achokmalit ishi na okla potta kat apihisashke.

SEK. 3. Nan ulhpisa ilappa akanima ho ik ai ahli cho hokmat nanik ai ulhpeyeso. Mako isht alhpisa cha nan isht imhlika kat ulhtoba osh onotolat atohobashke, yohmi kat tulli holisso $5.00 kano takla kiyokmat $25.00 kano ontia kiyo ho atoba shke, yohmik ma Chahta ai achuffa kiyo hosh holisso ishi osh nipi kanchi atokokmat o holisso ishi tok at i kobafash ki.

SEK. 4. Nan ulhpisa ilappat hlupulli makinli hosh ai ahlit kullot itoyola shke.

Nov. 13, 1890, miko aiokpachi.

W. N. JONES,
P. C. C. N.

BILL 15.

Chahta yakni ilappa i nan ulhtoka intruders aiima Atoksali yat akaniohma he otanichi nan ulhpesa.

Chahta Okla i nan upesa ittanaha chito ittafamat chiya ka yakohmit ulhpesashke.

Shalif ut imaiulhpiesa cha "Intruders" micha chahta ebabolhtina keyo nana akaniohmi ya miko chito imotanichi hachi kat Judge nana hohkia anumpa kallo imaicshi hosh Permit isha kiyo putta micha I Petition a hatak hohchifo atakohli aiɐlhpiesa tuka alotola hekeyo micha Shalif keyukmat nan ɐlhtoka nana hohkia nan Ulhpesa hosh amia ho "Intruders" micha chahta iba holh tina keyo aiimma atoksala chi hosh ɐlhtoka yosh Nation liappa kocha hea imanoachi toko ikaialho hokma miko chito yat imaiɐlhpiesa cha mehmakinli ho United States hatak ɐpi homma nana ishtimɐtta ya imanoachashki. Nan ɐlhpasa ilappat ameha kako iakaya hosh imannoah hokmat kanalla hea asilhhashki. Shalif kanim ma hohkia nan ɐlhpesa ilappat ameha ka ikaialho hokmat nan ɐlhpesa kobaffi isht ɐlhpesashki. Micha Circuit Court itikba yo anumpa isht aionotola hosh Tali holisso achpokoli Talhapi, ka ola kiyo hosh anoti Taliholisso Talhepa achaffa kano misha keyo hosh nana ai ikalho tuk putta ka isht aionotolashki Nan ɐlhpesa ilappat lhopulli hayat ai alhit holittopashki.

Nofimba 14, 1887, Aiokpachi.

THOMPSON McKINNEY,
Miko Chito.

(ENGLISH) BILL LXIV.*

An Act for the better securing the safety of the election returns in the election of Principal Chief, and of the National officers.

Be it enacted by the General Council of the Choctaw Nation assembled.

SECTION 1. That at every election for Principal Chief, or for any or all of the National officers, upon the delivery by the Sheriff or his deputy, to the proper Supreme Judge of the poll books of such Sheriff's county, said Judge shall give to such Sheriff a receipt, naming each poll book received, and particularly describing the same whether securely sealed, mutilated or not.

SEC. 2. The Supreme Judge shall at once deposit such poll books in a secure box or other safe receptacle, in which there shall be kept no other thing except the poll books containing the returns of election for Principal Chief, or for national officers. He shall retain said poll books in said box or receptacle, under lock and key, until such time as he is by law required to transmit them to the National Secretary. While said books are in his possession the Supreme Judge shall not exhibit the same to any one, nor permit any person, under any pretext, to inspect or to handle them.

SEC. 3. At the proper time such Judge shall, in person, take said poll books to the National Secretary, who shall give

---

*Skipped by mistake by the compilers and mistake noted just in time to insert here.

to such Judge receipts in all respects similar to those required herein to be given by the Supreme Judge to the various Sheriffs.

SEC. 4. Upon the delivery by the National Secretary to the Speaker of the House of such poll books, said Speaker shall give similar receipts to said Secretary.

SEC. 5. It shall be the duty of each Supreme Judge to preserve duplicates, made at the time, of all receipts so given by him to the various Sheriffs. These duplicates he shall deliver to said Speaker of the House in person, as soon as practicable after he has delivered the poll books to the National Secretary.

SEC. 6. In case any Supreme Judge is unable, by reason of sickness or other unavoidable casualty, to deliver the poll books and duplicate receipts in person to the National Secretary and Speaker of the House, respectively, as herein above required, then he shall at once notify the National Secretary of such inability. The National Secretary shall thereupon proceed in person to the place where such Supreme Judge may be, and then receive from him the poll books and duplicate receipts, and deliver to him receipts as herein above required, and the National Secretary shall then deliver the books and duplicate receipts to the Speaker, as aforesaid. In case of the inability of the National Secretary to act as provided in this section, then the President of the Senate shall designate some one of the national officers to act in his stead.

SEC. 7. And be it furthar enacted, That if any judge of election fail to certify to any poll books, or, after having certified thereto, refuse to deliver the same, in manner and form as prescribed by law, then, in either such event, he shall be deemed guilty of a felony, and he shall, upon indictment and conviction thereof, be punished by a fine of not less than one hundred dollars ($100) nor more than five hundred dollars ($500), and in case he fails to pay the fine assessed within one day, he shall receive not less than thirty-nine (39) nor more than one hundred lashes well laid on his bare back, and this act shall take effect and be in force from and after its passage.

APPROVED, November 13, 1890.

W. N. JONES, P. C. C. N.

THE CHOCTAW NATION

PASSED AT THE

SPECIAL SESSION OF THE GENERAL COUNCIL

CONVENED AT

TUSHKA HUMMA

APRIL 6, 1891, AND ADJOURNED APRIL 11, 1891.

LAWS OF THE CHOCTAW NATION.

CALLED SESSION, 1891.

NO. 1.

An act to establish two boarding schools, erect buildings, etc.

SECTION 1. Be it enacted by the General Council of the Choctaw Nation assembled, that the sum of not exceeding forty thousand dollars is hereby appropriated out of any money in the treasury, not otherwise appropriated, for the erection of two boarding school buildings in the Choctaw Nation, one for boys and one for girls, to be located by the full Board of Education.

SEC. 2. Be it further enacted, that the sum appropriated shall be divided equally for each of said buildings, and the capacity of each of said buildings to be sufficient to lodge and accommodate one hundred scholars. The material used in the construction of said buildings shall be under the control and supervision of the Board of Education. Said buildings to be heated by steam or hot water, and special attention be given to safety from fire.

SEC. 3. Be it further enacted, that for the purpose of securing the best model buildings the Board of Education is hereby authorized to advertise in some leading newspapers for plans and specifications, specifying each building and the general purpose for which they are required, and to receive and open bids and let contracts to the best and most responsible bidders, and shall require a bond from the contractors which shall contain the provisions and stipulations usually contained in such agreements, requiring first-class materials for the construction of said buildings, and to be done in a first-class workman-like manner, and the completion of the same by a fixed date with a penalty for each day said completion is delayed.

SEC. 4. Be it further enacted, that the Board of Education is hereby required as soon as practicable, after the passage of act, to make advertisement and bids to be received not later than June 1, 1891; and if a balance be left on hand of the appropriation after the completion of said buildings, said balance to be covered back into the National treasury, and this act take effect and be in force from and after its passage.

Approved April 4, 1891.

W. N. JONES, P. C. C. N.

NO. 2.

An act for the relief of certain Mississippi Choctaws.

Be it enacted by the General Council of the Choctaw Nation assembled, that the sum of two hundred and ninety-five dollars is hereby appropriated out of any money in the treasury, not otherwise appropriated, to reimburse Cornelius Hickman and family (4), Presley Isham and family (4), Nat Sakki (1), Dixon Ripley (1), Taylor Bell (1), Jane Sakki (1), Lee Nobbee (1), Tom Sakki and family (5), James Sakki (1), Allex Sakki (1), Isaac Simpson and family (5), and Matt Sakki and family (3), Choctaws (late arrivals from the State of Mississipi) for their expenditures while immigrating, and to enable them to obtain the necessaries of life, they having arrived too late last year to raise a crop of any kind; and this act shall take effect and be in force from and after its passage.

Approved April 4, 1891.

W. N. JONES, P. C. C. N.

NO. 3.

An act repealing an act in reference to Licensed Traders, approved November 4, 1890.

SECTION 1. Be it enacted by special session of the General Council of the Choctaw Nation assembled, that an act in reference to Licensed Traders, approved Nov. 4, 1890, be and the same is hereby repealed.

SEC. 2. Be it further enacted, that the act of November 1, 1883, in reference to Licensed Traders be and the same is hereby re-enacted and declared to be in force, and this act shall take effect and be in force from and after its passage.

Approved April 6, 1891.

W. N. JONES, P. C. C. N.

NO. 4.

An act requiring National Contractors to furnish transportation for Inspectors.

Whereas, it is necessary that the Inspector for the Choctaw Nation be present when every inspection of ties and measurement of lumber and all kinds of timber is had, and

Whereas, great numbers of ties and other timbers are brought to the track at points where there is no station, and

Whereas, it is a source of great inconvenience to said Inspectors on all the lines of railroads in this Nation to devise means for attending said inspections, therefore,

SECTION 1. Be it enacted by the General Council of the Choctaw Nation assembled, that the contractors for furnishing ties and timbers of all kinds to the several railroads running through this Nation are hereby required to furnish transportation for the several inspectors on the several railroads in this Nation in going to and from places of inspection.

SEC. 2. Be it further enacted, that all contractors for furnishing ties and timber of all kinds to the said railroads who shall fail or refuse to furnish such transportation for Inspectors shall forfeit their contracts; and this act shall take effect and be in force from and after its passage.

Approved April 6, 1891.

W. N. JONES, P. C. C. N.

NO. 5.

An act appropriating $750 for nine additional scholars at Armstrong Orphan School.

Be it enacted by the General Council of the Choctaw Nation assembled, that the sum of seven hundred and fifty dollars be and the same is hereby appropriated out of any money in the treasury, not otherwise appropriated, for the support of nine scholars at the Armstrong Orphan School, in addition to the number now allowed by law, and that this act shall take effect and be in force from and after its passage.

Approved April 6, 1891.

W. N. JONES, P. C. C. N.

NO. 6.

An act appropriating $2250 for the benefit of Armstrong Orphan School.

SECTION 1. Be it enacted by the General Council of the Choctaw Nation assembled, that the sum of two thousand two hundred and fifty dollars be and the same is hereby appropriated out of any money in the treasury not otherwise appropriated, in addition to the appropriation of seven thousand dollars heretofore passed, to-wit: November 3, 1890, for the erection of new building and for repairing the present one at Armstrong Orphan School.

SEC. 2. Be it further enacted, that all of this appropriation, or so much of it as is necessary, shall be expended under the supervision and with the consent of the Board of Education, and any balance left after the completion of the said building and repairs shall be turned into the treasury by the President of the Board of Education, and this act shall take effect and be in force from and after its passage.

Approved April 6, 1891.

W. N. JONES, P. C. C. N.

NO. 7.

SECTION 1. Be it enacted by the General Council of the Choctaw Nation assembled, that the privilege is hereby granted to Walter Patterson to turnpike and establish a toll-gate at a point on the Fort Smith and McAlister road, where said road crosses Gains creek, in Gains county, upon the following terms and conditions: That if said Walter Patterson turnpikes by grading the earth and leveling with stones the said road from where it crosses Gains creek westward to a distance of five miles he shall be entitled to demand and receive therefor, from all persons on the same, excepts citizens of this Nation, the rates of toll to-wit: For each four-wheel wagon, or other vehicle, drawn by four or more horses, mules or oxen, with driver, the sum of 50 cents; for each four-wheel wagon or other vehicle drawn by one or two horses, mules or oxen, with driver, 25 cents; for man and horse, 10 cents; each person on foot, 5 cents; for each animal in every drove of cattle, horses, mules, hogs or sheep 1 cent.

SEC. 2. Be it further enacted that privilege to receive toll herein given shall not take effect until said turnpike is completed, and shall continue in full force for the period of ten years, provided said turnpike shall be kept in good order and repairs; and all other persons are hereby prohibited from making any road across said creek for a distance of a mile up or down said creek.

SEC. 3. Be it further enacted, that if any person or persons, not citizens of this Nation, refuse to pay the aforesaid toll upon application, with proper proof being made to the United States Indian Agent for the Choctaw and Chickasaw, he shall take such steps as may be necessary to secure and collect the same.

SEC. 4. Be it further enacted, that this act shall take effect and be in force from and after its passage.

Approved April 8, 1891.

W. N. JONES, P. C. C. N.

NO. 8.

An act admitting certain Mississippi Indians to citizenship.

Be it enacted by the General Council of the Choctaw Nation assembled, that Mrs. Anna Boyd, Mrs. Lenas Southerland, Mrs. Ozie Travis, Mrs. M. William, Choctaws lately from the State of Mississippi,—and full sister of C. A. Bilbo who has been heretofore admitted—and their descendants be and they are hereby declared citizens of the Choctaw Nation.

Be it further enacted that this act take effect and be in force from and after its passage.

Approved April 8, 1891.

W. N. JONES, P. C. C. N.

NO. 9.

An act in relation to Peddlers and other traders herein mentioned.

SECTION 1. Be it enacted by the General Council of the Choctaw Nation assembled, that all non-citizens who desire to engage in the following businesses shall pay to the sheriff of the county wherein they propose to trade as follows, to-wit: Ice cream and lemonade stands at picnic $5.00 per day; ice cream and lemonade stands, in towns, $25.00 per year. Peddlers who travel in a wagon $25.00 per year; and pack peddlers $10 per year.

SEC. 2. Be it further enacted, that all non-citizens proposing to engage in such business, as above stated, shall first present a petition to the principal Chief, signed by five responsible citizens of this Nation. When he shall have obtained the permit he shall pay to the sheriff of the county wherein he proposes to trade the sum above stated, to be by him placed in the National treasury for National purposes. The said sheriff shall be entitled to 10 per cent. of all money collected by him under this law; and this act shall take effect and be in force from and after its passage.

Approved April 8, 1891.

W. N. JONES, P. C. C. N.

NO. 10.

An act appropriating $500 for five additional scholars at Wheelock Seminary.

Be it enacted by the General Council of the Choctaw Nation assembled, that the sum of five hundred dollars is hereby appropriated out of any money in the treasury, not otherwise appropriated, for the support of five additional scholars at Wheelock Seminary, to be paid on the certificate of the Superintendent of Wheelock Seminary, and this act shall take effect and be in force from and after its passage.

Approved April 8, 1891.

W. N. JONES, P. C. C. N.

NO. 11.

A Resolution asking pardon for Willie Anderson, of Jackson county, for assault with intent to kill.

Whereas, Willie Anderson, of Jackson county, was convicted for shooting, while intoxicated, a bullet into a Pullman car at Atoka, Choctaw Nation, and

Whereas, we sincerely believe that the striking of the car was entirely unintentional, and

Whereas, he has always been a good citizen, and we believe truly that he will never again err in such a manner, but if pardoned by his excellency, the President of the United States, will make a valuable citizen. Therefore

Be it resolved by the General Council of the Choctaw Nation assembled, that the President of the United States is hereby respectfully petitioned to grant the pardon of William Anderson, of Jackson county, and restore him to his family and people; and this resolution take effect and be in force from and after its passage.

Approved April 8, 1891.

W. N. JONES, P. C. C. N.

NO. 12.

An act providing that the compensation of local Trustees shall be continued for the current scholastic year.

Whereas, an act was passed by the General Council and approved November, 14, 1890, making an appropriation of fifteen hundred dollars to pay local Trustees in accordance with the old law, and

Whereas, an act was passed and approved October 31, 1890, depriving the local Trustees of the Choctaw Nation of their compensation after they had entered upon the performance of their duties. Therefore

Be it enacted by the General Council of the Choctaw Nation assembled, that the sum of fifteen hundred dollars, which was appropriated in the general appropriation bill of November 14, 1890, shall be expended in payment of local Trustees, the same as it would have been expended had not the school law of October 31, 1890, been passed; and this act shall take effect and be in force from and after its passage.

Approved April 8, 1891.

W. N. JONES, P. C. C. N.

NO. 13.

An act entitled an act regulating the time and manner of Sheriffs' making Reports to their respective County Treasurers, and for other purposes.

Be it enacted by the General Council of the Choctaw Nation assembled, that each and every Sheriff of this Nation is hereby required to make quarterly reports to their respective county Treasurer, exhibiting for his inspection all papers, permits, executions and other documents of whatsoever character remaining in his hands uncollected or served, and then and there turn over all funds belonging to his county to said Treasurer; and all funds due to the officers or other persons, such as fees, judgments, etc., taking their respective receipts. And failure on the part of any Sheriff, of this Nation, or refusal to comply with the foregoing, or attempt to withhold any funds due the county official or person to whom, by law the same is due, shall be construed as sufficient grounds for the vacation of his commission as Sheriff by the Principal Chief, who shall at once vacate the same upon the sworn statement of any county Treasurer, setting forth the facts that such Sheriff refuses, fails, or neglects to comply with the terms of this act.

SEC. 2. Be it further enacted that it shall be the duty of each County Treasurer, of this Nation, to carefully examine all papers, permits, executions and other documents in the hands of the Sheriff of their respective counties quarterly, when presented to him by said Sheriff, in compliance with Section 1, of this act, and if it should be found, after examination, that said Sheriff has fairly exhibited all papers in his office and duly turned over and accounted for all funds due the county of which he is Sheriff, he shall so certify in writing to that effect, and it shall be a receipt to the Sheriff for that quarter, provided, however, that the Sheriff's report and examination of the papers in his office together with the delivery of the county funds by said Sheriff to his respective County Treasurer shall be made in open County Court and under the suspervision of the County Judge, and the result of such examination, etc., be spread upon the minutes of said Court to be approved by said Judge. And provided further, that should the Treasurer find upon examination of any Sheriff's office that he is withholding funds due the county of which he may be Sheriff, it shall be his duty to so state to the Principal Chief under oath, setting forth the facts and amount of such shortage.

SEC. 3. Be it further enacted, that from and after the passage of this act it shall be unlawful for any Sheriff of this Nation to receive money and receipt for the same in lieu of a permit in any case before such permit shall have been applied for and issued. Every Sheriff violating this section shall be fined not less than twenty dollars for each and every offense upon conviction in the Circuit Court of his district. And such receipt or sworn testimony of the party to whom it was given shall be conclusive evidence against him.

SEC. 4. Be it further enacted, that the fees allowed by law to the County Clerks for the issuing of permits be and the same is hereby made payable out of the county treasury of their respective counties; and all acts and parts of acts heretofore enacted, coming in contact with with this act, are hereby repealed, and that this act take effect from and after its passage.

Approved April 8, 1891.

W. N. JONES, P. C. C. N.

NO. 14.

An act appropriating three thousand dollars for the benefit of Wheelock Orphan Seminary.

Be it enacted by the General Council of the Choctaw Nation assembled, that the sum of three thousand dollars is hereby appropriated out of any money in the treasury, not otherwise appropriated, to furnish steam heaters, furniture and repairing the said Seminary.

Be it further enacted, that all of this appropriation, or so much as is necessary, shall be expended under the supervision and consent of the Board of Education, and any balance on hand after the completion of said repairing and furnishing, etc., shall be turned into the treasury of the Choctaw Nation by the President of the Board of Education.

Be it further enacted, that this act shall take effect and be in force from and after its passage.

Approved April 8, 1891.

W. N. JONES, P. C. C. N.

NO. 15.

An act admitting certain Choctaws from Mississippi to citizenship in the Choctaw Nation.

Be it enacted by the General Council of the Choctaw Nation assembled, that Joe Willis and his children, Nancy Selan, and Frank Willis and his sister Liney Willis, and Billy Willis and his children Lee and Serena Willis, Thompson Barnett, James Sakki and Thomas Sakki, and Wallace Sam and his wife Fannie Sam and their children Milley, Jeruzy, Luke, Silley, Lizzie, Liza and Era Sam, all having just come from the old Nation in Mississippi, are hereby admitted to all of the rights and privileges of citizenship in the Choctaw Nation, and this act shall take effect and be in force from and after its passage.

Approved April 8, 1891.

W. N. JONES, P. C. C. N.

NO. 16.

An act recognizing the citizenship of certain Mississippi Choctaws.

Be it enacted by the General Council of the Choctaw Nation assembled, that following Mississippi Choctaws, late arrival, to-wit: 1 Cornelius Hickman, 2 Eliza Ann Hickman, 3 Jeff Hickman, 4 Presley Isham, 5 Ellen Isham, 6 William Isham, 7 Nat Sakki, 8 Dixon Ripley, 9 Taylor Bell, 10 Alex Sakki, 11 Jane Sakki, 12 Lee Nobbe, 13 Henson Haltenstyle, 14, Phœbe Haltenstyle, 15 Milton Haltenstyle, 16 Jesse Haltenstyle, 17 Fall Haltenstyle are hereby recognized as citizens of this Nation and are entitled to all the rights, privileges and immunities of other citizens of this Nation; and this act take effeect and be in force from and after its passage.

Approved April 9, 1891.

W. N. JONES, P. C. C. N.

NO. 17.

An act for the relief of certain Mississippi Choctaws.

Be it enacted by the General Council of the Choctaw Nation

assembled, that the sum of $300 be and the same is hereby appropriated out of any money in the treasury, not otherwise appropriated, as a relief for the following late arrivals from Missisipi, to-wit: 1 Joe Willis, 2 Nancy Willis, 3 Frank Willis, 4 Liney Willis, 5 Billy Willis, 6 Liza Willis, 7 Serena Willis, 8 Thompson Burney, 9 Wallace Sam, 10 Fannie Sam, 11 Jemzy Sam, 12 Luke Sam 13 Sally Sam, 14 Liza Sam, 15 Lizzie Sam, 16 Asa Sam, 17 Henson Haltenstyle, 18 Phœbe Haltenstyle, 18 Milton Haltenstyle, 20 JesseHaltenstyle, 21 Fall Haltenstyle, 22 Sanders Amos, 23 William Amos, 24 Ann Amos, 25 John Amos, 26 Soloman Amos, 27 Puss Amos, 28 Casson Wilson, 29 Belson Wilson, 30 Medarial Wilson; and this act to take effect and be in force from and after its passage.

Approved April 9, 1891.

W. N. JONES, P. C. C. N.

NO. 18.

Whereas, the Glen and Tucker families now residing in the Choctaw Nation and claiming citizenship, whose cases have been decided adversely and are now pending before the Department at Washington, and

Whereas, the General Council are thoroughly satisfied that said families are not of Choctaw descent. Therefore

SECTION 1. Be it enacted by the General Council of the Choctaw Nation assembled, that the sum of ($5000) five thousand dollars is hereby appropriated out of any money in the treasury, not otherwise appropriated, to enable the Principal Chief to successfully resist their application for citizenship, by employing able counsel to protect and defend the Choctaw Nation in said appeal cases; and this act to take effect and be in force from and after its passage.

Approved April 9, 1891.

W. N. JONES, P. C. C. N.

NO. 19.

An act making an appropriation to pay outstanding school certificates of Peter Garland, late Trustee of the First District.

SECTION 1. Be it enacted by the General Council of the Choctaw Nation assembled, that whereas there appears numerous certificates of indebtedness issued by Peter Garland, late trustee of the first District outstanding against the Nation, the exact amount not known; therefore, there is hereby appropriated out of any money in the treasury, not otherwise appropriated, a sum sufficient to pay said certificates, and upon presentation, no doubt appearing as to genuineness, the Treasurer shall pay the same.

SEC. 2. That this act take effect and be in force from and after its passage.

Approved April 9, 1891.

W. N. JONES, P. C. C. N.

NO. 20.

An act authorizing a release of all the title and interest that the Choctaws have in the Cheyenne and Arraphoe lands lying south of the Canadian River and west of the 98 degree of west longitude, and making conveyance thereof.

Be it enacted by the General Council of the Choctaw Nation assembled, that the delegation of 1889, to-wit: J. S. Standley, H. C. Harris and R. J. Ward, and Green McCurtain, National Treasurer, and some one to be appointed by the Principal Chief with the advice and consent of the Senate and commissioned by the Principal Chief, are hereby empowered, authorized and directed to proceed to Washington City, D. C., and as delegates specially authorized thereto, execute releases and conveyances and transfer to the United States all the right, title and interest of the Choctaw Nation to their lands lying west of the 98 degree of west longitude and south of the Canadian River and now occupied by the Cheyenne and Arraphoe tribe of Indians, for the payment of which an act of Congress of the United States was approved March 3, 1891; and this act take effect and be in force from and after its passage.

Approved April 9, 1891.

W. N. JONES, P. C. C. N.

NO. 21.

An act making requisition for the sum of $2,243.587.50, due the Choctaw Nation under an act of Congress, approved March 3, 1891.

Be it enacted by the General Council of the Choctaw Nation assembled, that the delegation of 1889, the National Treasurer of the Choctaw Nation and some one to be selected and commissioned by the Principal Chief, with the advice and consent of the Senate, are hereby authorized and directed to proceed to Washington City, D. C., and make a requsition on the government of the United States in such manner and form as may be satisfactory to the proper authorities of the United States for the sum of $2,243,587.50, being three-fourths of the sum of $2,991,450 appropriated by the act of the Congress of the United States, approved March 3, 1891, in payment of the interest of the Choctaw and Chickasaw Nations in the lands west of 98th degree of west longitude; and the National Treasurer shall deposit the same in some responsible bank or banks, subject to the order of the Choctaw Nation, and such bank or banks to give a bond payable to the Choctaw Nation in a sum equal to the amount so deposited. Such bond to be approved by the National Treasurer and to be recovered by the National Treasurer for the use and benefit of the Choctaw Nation and conditioned as other bonds are conditioned for like purposes; and this act shall take effect and be in force from and after its passage.

Approved April 9, 1891.

W. N. JONES, P. C. C. N.

NO. 22.

An act making an appropriation for the relief of J. S. Standley.

Be it enacted by the General Council of the Choctaw Nation assembled, that the sum of ($750) seven hundred and fifty dollars is hereby appropriated out of any money in the treasury, not otherwise appropriated to pay J. S. Standley for services in recovering ($15,000) fifteen thousand dollars for the Choctaw Nation, and the National Auditor is hereby authorized to issue his warrant on the National Treasurer for the amount. That this act take effect and be in force from and after its passage.

Approved April 9, 1891.

W. N. JONES, P. C. C. N.

NO. 23.

An act authorizing settlement with the delegation for services rendered in the prosecution of the claim of the Choctaw Nation in the Leased District.

Be it enacted by the General Council of the Choctaw Nation assembled, that the National Treasurer is hereby authorized and directed (as soon as practicable after the receipt of the Leased District money) to make a settlement with the delegation as per act of the General Council of the Choctaw Nation, approved December 24, 1889, and to pay over to them such sum or sums as may be due them; and that this act shall take effect and be in force from after its passage.

Approved April 10, 1891.

W. N. JONES, P. C. C. N.

NO. 24.

An act to authorize the Principal Chief to purchase carpets and have the roof of the Capitol repaired.

SECTION 1. Be it enacted by the General Council of the Choctaw Nation assembled, that the Principal Chief is hereby authorized to contract with some responsible party to furnish a suitable carpet for the floors of the Senate hall and the House of Representatives, also to repair the roof of the Capitol building.

SEC. 2. Be it further enacted, that in order to carry out the provisions of Section 1 of this act the Principal Chief is hereby authorized to draw on the National Treasurer for the amount of his expenditures, and make a detailed report thereof to the next General Council; and this act shall take effect from and after its passage.

Approved April 10, 1891.

W. N. JONES, P. C. C. N.

NO. 25.

An act changing an election Precinct in San Bois county.

Be it enacted by the General Council of the Choctaw Nation assembled, that the election precinct in San Bois county, known as Kulli Chito Precinct, be and the same is hereby removed and located at Jerry Folsom's place, two miles south, and to be called and known as Oak Hill Election Precinct; and all future elections shall be held there; and this act shall take effect and be in force from and after its passage.

Approved April 10, 1891.

W. N. JONES, P. C. C. N.

NO. 26.

An act authorizing distribution per capita of the money due the the Choctaw Nation for the sale of a portion of the leased district under act of Congress; approved March 3, A. D. 1891.

SECTION 1. Be it enacted by the General Council of the Choctaw Nation asaembled, that the sum of one million six hundred and fifty-seven thousand six hundred and ninety-one dollars ($1,657,691) being the balance, after deducting delegates per cent, and twenty-five thousand and five dollars for necessary expense in procuring and distributing the same, shall be paid out *per capita* among Choctaw citizens by blood residing in the Choctaw and Chickasaw Nation at the date of this act.

SEC. 2. That for properly executing Section 1, of this act, it shall be the duty of the Principal Chief to appoint three commissioners for each county in the Choctaw Nation and three for the Chickasaw District, whose duty shall be to enroll all the names on rolls to be prepared for the purpose under order of the Chief; the beneficiaries under this act when said rolls are completed, which shall be done as speedily as possible, they shall be carried by one of the commissioners to Tashka Humma and delivered to a committee consisting of the Principal Chief, Secretary, Auditor and Treasurer who shall ascertain exactly the amount due each person, whereupon the Treasurer shall proceed to disburse the same, commencing in the Second District; the payment to be made at the District Court ground of each District. The Auditor shall accompany the Treasurer and verify the payments. The Light Horse shall also attend as a guard. The Principal Chief, if he desires, may superintend the disbursement in person.

SEC. 3. The Commissioners shall be sworn by some county judge which oath shall be endorsed on their appointment and shall complete their work in not less than twenty days. They shall meet at the most public place for convenience of the people in their respective counties, and shall receive the sum of one hundred and fifty dollars each for their services.

SEC. 4. The Principal Chief, shall notify the Commissioners when to begin work, soon after receiving the money; and this act take effect and be in force from and after its passage.

Approved April 11, 1891.

W. N. JONES, P. C. C. N.

NO. 27.

An act granting to John E. McBrayer a Ferry on the Arkansas River.

Be it enacted by the General Council of the Choctaw Nation assembled, that John E. McBrayer, a citizen of the Choctaw Nation, residing at Tamaha in San Bois county, is hereby authorized and permitted to establish and operate a Ferry at Pleasant Bluff, on the Arkansas River, the said McBrayer being the owner of the premises on the Choctaw side adjoining the landing. This privilege shall continue for the period of ten years, extend up and down the said river for the distance of one mile each way. Said McBrayer to keep the banks and approaches to the ferry, and his ferry boats in good condition, and the Choctaw Nation to be in no way responsible or liable to any party for loss or damage by reason of said ferry. Said McBrayer shall have the right to charge for vehicles drawn by more than two horses, mules or oxen, seventy-five cents; for vehicles drawn by two horses, mules or oxen, fifty cents; for vehicles drawn by a single animal thirty-five cents; for each animal, horses, mules or cattle, besides those drawing vehicles, ten cents; for each person on horse-back, twenty-five cents; for each person on foot, ten cents; for each hog or sheep, five cents; and this act shall take effect and be in force from and after its passage.

Approved April 11, 1891.

W. N. JONES, P. C. C. H.

NO. 28.

An act making an appropriation for expenses of extra Session of General Council.

Be it enacted by the General Council of the Choctaw Nation assembled, that the sum of ($4500) four thousand and five hundred dollars, or so much thereof as may be necessary, is hereby appropriated out of any money, not otherwise appropriated in the National treasury, to pay the the expenses of the extra session of the General Council, held in April, 1891; and this act shall take effect and be in force from and after its passage.

Approved April 11, 1891.

W. N. JONES, P. C. C. N.

NO. 29.

An act for the protection of the interest of Orphans in the money arising from the sale of the Leased District under act of Congress, approved March 3, 1891.

SECTION 1. Be it enacted by the General Council of the Choctaw Nation assembled, that the gross amount ascertained to be due the orphans now at Armstrong and Wheelock, arising under *per capita* distribution of the Leased District money, under act of Congress, approved March 3, 1891, shall be covered into the National Treasury and so entered on the books thereof, and shall draw interest at the rate of four per cent. per annum.

SEC. 2. That a list of said orphans shall be filed in the Auditor and Treasurer's office with the age of each orphan, and upon becoming of age of any orphan herein provided for, it shall be the duty of the National Auditor, without further action of the General Council, upon proper application to issue his warrant on the Treasurer for the said orphan's prorata of said sum with the accrued interest thereon.

SEC. 3. That this act take effect and be in force from and after its passage.

Approved April 11, 1891.

W. N. JONES, P. C. C. N.

NO. 30.

An act authorizing the Principal Chief to accompany the Special Delegation to Washington City, D. C.

Be it enacted by the General Council of the Choctaw Nation assembled, that Wilson N. Jones, Principal Chief, shall accompany the special delegation to Washington City, D. C., and shall sign officially with the delegation the release of the interest of the Choctaw Nation in the lands west of 78 degrees west longitude as contemplated in the act of the Congrees of the United States, approved March 3, 1891; and shall also sign with Special Delegation the requisition for the monies due for said lands; *provided, however*, if from any disability he should be unable to accompany the delegation or should be unable to act, then the delegation are authorized to continue the business; and this act shall take effect and be in force from and after its passage.

It became a law by its own limitation.

NO. 31.

A resolution of adjournment.

Be it resolved by the Special Session of the General Council of the Choctaw Nation assembled, that the Special Session of the Choctaw nation (now in session) shall adjourn on Saturday the 11th day of April, A. D. 1891, at 3'clock p. m., and that this resolution shall take effect from and after its passage.

NO. 32.

An act providing pay for the Special Delegates to Washington City, D. C., to sign release of the Leased District and make requisition for monie arising therefrom.

SECTION 1. Be it enacted by the General Council of the Choctaw Nation assembled, that the Special Delegation to Washton City, D. C., are to be paid as follows, to-wit: The expenses of W. N. Jones, Principal Chief, and Green McCurtain, National Treasurer, are to be paid, they being salaried officers, and the other, who is to be appointed and confirmed, shall receive for his services five hundred dollars and his expenses actually incurred while in the performance of his mission; *provided, however*, the said appointee is not a salaried officer, in which case his expenses alone shall be paid, and the National Treasurer shall pay the same on the order of the Principal Chief.

SEC. 2. Be it further enacted, that the delegation of 1889, tow-it : J. S. Standley, H.C. Harris and R. J. Ward shall not be entitled to any per diem or expense funds; and that this act shall take effect and be in force from and after its passage.

It became a law by its own limitation.

This is to certify that the above is a true and correct copy of the original acts now on file in my office.

Witness my hand and the great seal of the Choctaw Nation. Done at Tashka Humma, this the 24th day of June A. D., 1891.

J. B. JACKSON,
National Secretary Choctaw Nation.